T0090429

CELEBRATING LITERACY IN THE RWENZORI REGION

Lest we Forget

*A biographical narrative of Uganda's youngest
Member of Parliament 1980-85*

Amos Mubunga Kambere

Order this book online at www.trafford.com
or email orders@trafford.com

Most Trafford titles are also available at major online book retailers.

© Copyright 2010 Amos Mubunga Kambere.
All rights reserved. No part of this publication may be reproduced, stored in a retrieval system, or
transmitted, in any form or by any means, electronic, mechanical, photocopying, recording, or
otherwise, without the written prior permission of the author.

Printed in Victoria, BC, Canada.

ISBN: 978-1-4269-3097-3 (sc)

ISBN: 978-1-4269-3098-0 (hc)

ISBN: 978-1-4269-3099-7 (e-book)

Library of Congress Control Number: 2010906829

*Our mission is to efficiently provide the world's finest, most comprehensive book publishing
service, enabling every author to experience success. To find out how to publish your
book, your way, and have it available worldwide, visit us online at www.trafford.com*

Trafford rev. 5/14/2010

 www.trafford.com

North America & international
toll-free: 1 888 232 4444 (USA & Canada)
phone: 250 383 6864 ♦ fax: 812 355 4082

FOREWORD

Lest we forget indeed! The immediate aftermath of the active militant Rwenzururu struggle saw a phenomenal awakening in development in the Rwenzori region as a whole. The most glaring example of such progress was in the field of education. Through collaborative effort on the part of the politicians, the technocrats and the entire population, a lot was achieved. In four short years, there were eight Government grant-aided secondary schools (in place of one), two partially grant-aided secondary schools and one private secondary school; two primary teacher training colleges and a technical school. One of the secondary schools was A-level status.

In this short narrative, the writer has labored to relate the process by which these achievements were made and enriched it by making it a personal autobiography. It becomes all the more important when it is borne in mind that he was the youngest member of the 3rd parliament of Uganda during this phenomenal period.

While it is not strictly a historical narrative, it certainly is historic. It at once brings into view the status of education in the region on the eve of Uganda's independence and explains that *status quo*. It is the work of a teacher-cum-politician and of necessity, it combines both. As a teacher, he orders his story while as a politician, he highlights selected aspects.

Whereas the geographical scope is the Rwenzori region, more attention is given to the writer's zone of jurisdiction, Kasese. But the reader should generalize for Bundibugyo, bearing in mind that the cause of the bitterness covered the whole region.

The stage is systematically set to prepare for both the development of the region and the autobiography. No development could have taken place when the local people were not in control of their own destiny. Nor could it take place when there was war going on. So peace had to be sought after first. This search for peace was ironically characterized by violence. The process brought on the scene two young men who tirelessly worked to bring about peace.

Unfortunately their continued development efforts were terminated by events at national level. It is this stage that the autobiography takes centre stage. The personal suffering that Amos suffered made him look at life differently. He receives a baptism of fire through which he relocates both spiritually and physically. This relocation offers the necessary peace and facilitation to produce this work.

Celebrating Literacy in the Rwenzori region is an eye-opener to all the people in the region. With collaborative effort and stamina God will always bless our efforts.

Enoch Sekalombi Muhindo

Acknowlegement and Dedication

This book is dedicated to my grand mother Georgina, my mother Julia, and my wife Edith Kambere who pray for my family unceasingly.

I would like to acknowledge and thank King Charles for providing me with accurate information regarding his father the late Isaya. I want to thank Jim Enoch Muhindo for being there during the hard times of developing our developmental programs, Sande Nelson, Eva Bwambale, Dr.Syahuka-Muhindo Rev. Nelson Baliira, young Dan Kashagama for encouraging me to write this book after listening to a short story about Kasese Elections, and all those I might have asked a few questions regarding the work of this book. You are all appreciated. Finally to my father Fenehasi Mubunga who went with me on the gateway train to the city to seek an education that my district could not provide.

INTRODUCTION

This book is written and dedicated to the people of Kasese and Bundibugyo Districts, found on the foothills of the Mountains of the Moon. The people of this region covering the entire mountain range in both Uganda and the Democratic Republic of Congo, suffered greatly during the colonial period from the early 1890s to the early 1960s. In Uganda especially, this suffering was characterized by discrimination, segregation, marginalization and general neglect in all aspects of life. Education which was used as a vehicle of social change elsewhere in the country was deliberately denied.

On the eve of national independence in 1962 the people of the region demanded for self determination by getting separated from the Toro kingdom administration under which the British had colonized them. Unfortunately the colonial government was too busy working out the modalities of ending their rule, to pay appropriate attention to this demand. This forced the people of the region into outright armed rebellion that was to last for twenty years.

In 1982 the leaders of the armed rebellion changed their method of struggle, ending twenty years of bitterness. The four short years that followed saw unprecedented development in many aspects of the social well being of the people in the region and most especially in the field of education.

The world is enormous, and everything we do to create a worldwide view broadens our horizons, and our choices for living and learning. Expanding our scope of thinking and learning makes life more fun and worth of a living. This can only be achieved through education and, denying education to the people of the Ruwenzori was to limit their horizons and even their perception of themselves as human beings. This book will try to explain the circumstances that led to this plight.

The people on the slopes of Mt. Rwenzori [internationally known as the Mountains of the Moon], lived in their small world, narrow in scope and restricted in its consciousness, limited in its horizons, so that in effect, they created a little universe of their own. It was quite easy to live in a small confined, self-centered world. And, it was safe to exist this way before the intrusion of colonization from Europe. However, as soon as the rebellion opened their eyes the people became more aware and their perception suddenly became wider; learning became fun and later became the catalyst for widening their scope of perceiving things. The more learning became paramount in the lives of the people, the more vibrant the society became. Learning was the noble chariot of broadening this scope and was ushered in by leaders who came with vision and pragmatism.

I will also discuss the emergence of a new breed of leadership after the 20 years of war, which ushered in an era of political dialogue that brought down the rebellion peacefully and embarked on discerning areas of concern to the population. Emphasis on the introduction of educational institutions was the focus of the new leadership, and a challenge was set for those to continue with the banner of leadership, to water the seed so planted, to enable it bear fruit. The result was the explosion of education as the figures will show in this book.

This is in no way fiction or historical legend. It is the story of one young individual, who lived through it all, grew to become the youngest Member of Parliament in the central government of the Republic of Uganda and later left the scene unceremoniously. He lived to tell the story so that the next generation can sieve out lessons to be learned and to be told to the young people of this region.

In the later part of this narrative, we will see how twenty five cents was significant in shaping the leadership style of this 26 year old Member of Parliament. During the process of leaving the scene, after a humble 4 years in service, he was blessed with five US dollars which carried him to North America to live, settle, prosper and raise a family on hope, trusting in the mercies of the living God. At the end of this writing we will see the truth behind the myth unfold into reality and finally a kingdom of the people achieved.

Amos Mubunga Kambere

CHAPTER 1

On 30th of June, in the year of our Lord Nineteen hundred and sixty two, on a bright sunny Saturday afternoon, a declaration of independence was made by Isaya Mukirane, the then leader of the Rwenzururu Movement government. A three colored flag of yellow, green and white was hoisted at the headquarters of the Kingdom and an anthem already composed was sang by those who assembled to witness the occasion. The movement that included all the people of the mountain range constituted itself into an army of spears and sticks bearers, ready to liberate the entire mountain region from the leadership of the Toro Kingdom. Mr. Isaya Mukirane, the self-declared president, later became the King of the Kingdom after a declaration of secession from the Toro Kingdom, which was led by the "Omukama Rukira Basaija" of Toro. It is important to note here that the declaration of independence by Isaya came on 30th of June 1962 more than three months before Uganda acquired her own independence on October 9, 1962.

While Dr. Apollo Milton Obote was in London negotiating the instruments of independence for Uganda, the local leadership in the Toro Kingdom was behind closed doors embroidered in a constitution crisis in which they had denied recognition of the

1

Bakonzo and Bamba tribes as separate tribes in the constitution. The Rukurato [Toro parliament] had refused to include Lukonzo and Rwamba languages as languages that existed within the Kingdom. The representatives of the Bamba and Bakonzo in this Rukurato had subsequently walked out of this unprecedented meeting. Among those who walked out of this Rukurato were Kawamara Yeremia, Peter Mupalia, Bazarabusa and Isaya Mukirane. Isaya later became the leader of the rebellion. A few of the Bakonzo representatives like Erisa Nzige did not walk out of the Rukurato. They were later made ministers in the Omukama's government in which the Bakonzo and Bamba were not recognized according to the constitution of Uganda which Dr. Obote carried with him to London to negotiate for Uganda's independence from the United Kingdom.

The Bakonzo and Bamba are the aborigines of the then Toro and it was inconceivable that they could be denied the right to exist in the Uganda constitution. This constitution stipulated that all people living in Toro district were Batoro.

Toro kingdom had been formed in 1830 by one Prince Olimi Kaboyo, who had rebelled against his father, the King of Bunyoro Kitara. This young rebel prince had fled from Bunyoro to hide in the Mountains of the Moon which were inhabited by Bamba and Bakonzo. The Bakonzo had hidden this rebel King, whose heirs later turned against them and made them slaves. Despite the fact that all the inhabitants of Toro at the time were illiterate, all the available positions in the administration of the kingdom were to be given to Batoro when Toro was annexed to the British protectorate of Uganda by one Captain Lugard in 1893. The Bakonzo and Bamba became forced servants of the Batoro as a matter of policy. This caused much suffering and indignation among the Bakonzo and Bamba communities who made several attempts to liberate themselves. They staged a rebellion in 1919 led at this time by Nyamutswa, Tibamwenda and Kapoli. The Batoro leadership under the Omukama whose grandfather the Bakonzo had hidden in the mountain caves, arrested these three men, tortured them, and later killed them by hanging and burying them in one grave at Kagando, in Kisinga, the present site of Kagando Hospital.

Education and medical facilities were introduced in the Kingdom as I will discuss later in this book, but none were extended to Bamba and Bakonzo areas until the 1950s.

In 1961, the Bakonzo were allowed to send representatives to the Rukurato [Toro Parliament] and they used this chance to demand their inclusion in the Toro Constitution, which was rejected outright. When the matter was brought to the Governor General in Entebbe, the grievances were noted and confirmed as true. This caused more bad blood between the Batoro and the Bakonzo- Bamba leaders forcing the latter to walk as it was useless to sit in a parliament whose constitution did not recognize their existence. This resulted in killings in large numbers of our people, and the whole of 1962 saw the counties of Busongora, Bwamba, Burahya and Bunyangabu declared as disturbed areas. This was then the birth and entrenchment of the Rwenzururu Movement.

CHAPTER 2

July 10, 1962 was a busy Tuesday. It was a designated market day for the sub-county of Kyarumba where I was born. I was at that time in the market sitting beside my mother Julia who was selling banana juice [omubisi]. At about 12 noon, on that bright sunny day, about 10 Rwenzururu soldiers armed with mere sticks arrived in the market and started hitting the ground with their sticks while shouting *"Rwenzururu, Rwenzururu, Rwenzururu"* in unison. The market venders quickly dispersed and people took to their heels running for their lives. It had been common practice that if you heard men shouting the words "Rwenzururu", there was troubles to follow. These ten men expected people to reply in chorus as they shouted Rwenzururu. Failure to shout with them would result in being beaten up. Joining the chanting men was a sign of support for the declaration of independence, which had been announced two weeks earlier on 30 June, 1962. The Rwenzururu commanders at this time were targeting market places and churches on Sundays to send their message across. The declaration of independence by Isaya revitalized the morale of the Bakonzo and Bamba into a bitter struggle that was to last more than 20 years.

On that July tuesday, my mother and I left the juice unattended to and took off like every one else. As we fled, most of us had to join in the chorus of the Rwenzururu song to avoid retribution by the soldiers who could follow any direction. The trading center quickly came to a stand still and the local shops closed as the soldiers headed for the sub county [Gombolola] headquarters. The Chief at this sub-county was a Mutoro appointed by the Omukama of Toro. His name was Rwakijuma. The soldiers armed with sticks and pangas moved into the sub county headquarters, ransacked it and set the buildings on fire. The grass thatched ones around quickly vanished in flames while the permanent buildings were engulfed in smoke. Mr. Rwakijuma fled the scene and was never to be heard of again. He was believed to be armed with a rifle given to him by the Toro Kingdom assisted by the British who were still in charge as Uganda was not yet independent. It is interesting to note that Isaya declared Rwenzururu independent from Toro Kingdom before the entire Uganda became independent from the United Kingdom.

The uprising quickly spread throughout Bukonzo County. In Kisinga, on the following Friday, was a market day too. A different band of soldiers armed with spears and sticks arrived there, this time round mobilizing the Bakonzo from the market and matching towards the sub county [Gombolola] headquarters, which was some 300 meters away from the market. All in all, about 200 people matched towards the house of the gombolola chief, a Mutoro, with intentions of killing him and putting the house on fire. Not surprisingly this chief was armed with a shot gun. His name was Bamuloho. He fired through the window in self-defense, killing one of the Bakonzo demonstrators and managing to disperse the crowd. As they left the scene, they vandalized bridges, and torched Batoro houses as they fled back to the mountains shouting "Rwenzururu oye". These attacks spread in the entire region. On the side of the Toro area, the Batoro were attacking Bakonzo households in revenge and this caused an exodus of Bakonzo and Bamba and brought everything to a standstill. The following month saw the rebellion spread into Muhokya in Busongora. About 400 men armed with pangas and spears damaged property in the trading center and at the gombolola headquarters. During this riotous incident the police shot one Mukonzo.

5

Another group of Rwenzururu men infiltrated up to the omukama's palace. They were however apprehended before they made a disastrous move. One of the ideas they wanted to implement here was to infiltrate the enemy camp. They needed to outwit the enemy by mounting a solid intelligence from inside his own camp. This way they would have overrun the palace and taken it over; probably killing the "omukama" king.

These bands of people were not educated and basically depended on oral communications. But of course one can not assume that they were retarded. Whether they used oral or written language their intelligence, cause and determination could not be underestimated or deterred.

* * *

While I could afford to miss school on a Tuesday morning to help my mother carry stuff to the market, I could not afford to be away on other days of the week. The following week I had to routinely go to school. As the disturbances raged on, some schools in the area were closed either because the teachers fled for their lives or some were simply arrested and could not perform their duties. Most of the teachers were Batoro just as were the chiefs. At this time the entire mountain region had been declared a disturbed area and a state of emergency had been declared. In February 1963 an elected member of the first parliament Mr. Ezironi Bwambale was picked up from Kinyamaseke as he was talking to farmers who had come to sell their cotton produce. Rwenzururu soldiers kidnapped him, took him up hill up to Kabingo. When they could not carry him further up the hill, they stabbed him in the chest and left him in the valley either to die or to be rescued by the government troops who had immediately mounted a man search for him. Isaya Mukirane, the Rwenzururu president had ordered that Bwambale be brought before his council court to answer charges as to why he had decided to side with the Toro leadership and not introduced a motion in parliament seeking for a separate district for his people. Isaya still believed that a democratic process should have been followed to deal with the issues, which had led him, and his group to walk out of the "Rukurato". Bwambale was a member of the opposition Democratic Party that did not have a big say in the parliamentary decisions. Bwambale too, feared retribution from his constituency, which was largely dominated by Batoro voters who mostly lived on the lower lands of the mountain. Bwambale hailed from Bwera and most of his support was from Nyakatonzi, Katwe, Kilembe, Muhokya, Hima and Rwimi areas which had a large population of Batooro and most of whom were strong supporters of the Democratic Party, which sat on the opposition in the Uganda central government. Isaya accused Bwambale of not introducing a motion in parliament seeking the redress of the Bakonzo tribal issues. Isaya did not realize that Bwambale had just been elected, had not even made his maiden speech in parliament and besides he was on the opposition.

Bwambale was rescued by helicopter; alive bleeding and taken to Kilembe mines hospital for treatment; until the ministry of internal affairs ordered his transfer to Mulago hospital in Kampala. He was transported by police helicopter. At this point the Bakonzo and Bamba were dominated by sadness, deep frustrations as they asked questions why their basic human rights were being violated even by the central government, for which they had send an elected Mukonzo from which they thought solace would come. The infrastructure had broken down; schools and healthy centers had closed down. With the kidnapping and consequently the stabbing of a Member of Parliament, the Prime Minister, Dr. A Milton Obote had had no choice other than declaring the Rwenzuru secessionist movement to be a "dangerous movement to peace and order".

The Prime Minister and the Governor-general were quoted in the Uganda Argus, the government newspaper of February 18, 1963 as saying "the Rwenzururu movement has disgraced Uganda in the eyes of the world". Indeed as disturbances increased unabated, it was increasingly clear that the central government was failing to bring the rebellion to an end. This grossly hampered the delivery of services to the people. However, the Rwenzururu leadership and the people who now entirely supported the movement did not care about services especially when they knew that the Toro Kingdom government was violating their human rights. The Bakonzo and Bamba had vowed that it is better to perish than live in slavery. This was the guiding principle that kept the fire burning in all Rwenzururu-dominated areas. The central government, in their own desperation were scared that the situation was getting out of hand. They wanted to recapture their image in the eyes of the international community.

At this point they allowed Mr. Tom Stacey, a British writer and journalist who had written a few books about the mountains of the moon and the Rwenzururu movement, to come and meet with the Rwenzururu King. The central government now had to depend on Mr. Stacey to salvage their image by probably convincing Mukirane to abandon the rebellion and surrender. Mr. Stacey was able to meet with Isaya Mikirane in February 1963. He was the first negotiator appointed by the Ugandan government to attempt to end the movement, but his mission failed miserably and Isaya and his leadership moved further in the mountains in what was considered as the "furthest private cave".

Tom Stacey

The central government had deployed heavily by sending two companies of the Uganda Rifles who were already moving into the mountains with the help of local porters. As they moved about the mountains they were burning Bakonzo huts, houses and destroying property in a bid to cut off communication between the local Bakonzo and the Rwenzururu leadership.

Mr. Tom Stacey became a frequent visitor to the mountains because he had developed a personal relationship with the Rwenzururu people and their leadership. On most occasions he was mistakenly called "Isemusoki" a name which was given to another white man, who worked in Bwamba. Isemusoki, the husband to Nyamusoki lives in Norway while Kirstern Alnaes – Nyamusoki lives in London. This couple lived and worked extensively in Bwamba, had their first born baby girl after consulting a local medicine man in Bwamba who told them to name their first child Musoki if she was a girl. Because she lived with the Bamba for a long time and wrote books about the cultures of the Bamba and Bakonzo, she became famous. So when Tom Stacey returned to the Rwenzoris, the Bakonzo not knowing the difference between white people [*muzungus*] just called him Isemusoki. In the mean time, the leadership of the Rwenzururu, called him "Musabuli" which meant savior, because they liken him to "Jesus who came to save sinner". The fact that a white man could come all the way from London and side with the cause of the Bakonzo and Bamba was equivalent to being a savior, hence the name of Musabuli. One of the factors about Tom which impressed the Mukirane leadership was that as he traveled through the mountains, he knew where the army deployments were and was able to go warning Bakonzo natives of the dangers that were coming along. He was also able to tell the Rwenzuru leadership of how they were being sought by the advancing army. This enabled them to move into their furthest private cave. Today, this Tom Stacey has remained a 'legend' or is he, among the Bakonzo people. He is still accorded the dignity of a Musabuli especially when people think of his initiative to bring to the attention of the central government the plight of the Banyarwenzururu. Mr. Stacey's mission failed simply because he came from a democracy and when he heard the plight of the Bakonzo, read copies of their several memoranda to the government, he could not then ask them to surrender. He quickly grasped their concept of human rights violation, he grieved with them and instead of becoming a negotiator, he became an ally. In March 1963 after Tom Stacey had failed to bring the rebellion to reasonable understanding with the government, a white paper was issued recognizing what the commission of inquiry had recommended... "That seceding from Toro by the Bakonzo and Bamba was not acceptable". The white paper reaffirmed the emergency measures to continue until law and order was re-established. The white paper says "the Government realizes that its decisions will not satisfy the *extreme demands* of some Bamba and Bakonzo who want to secede from Toro and establish a separate district. But it trusts that these tribes and the people of Toro and the Omukama's government will loyally accept the central government's decisions". [Uganda Argus march26, 1963] For the government white paper to refer to us as "these tribes" while referring to the Batoro as the "people of Toro" clearly indicated that the government condoned the gross violation of the human rights of our people. Therefore there was necessary cause to be part of the rebellion.

This assertion by the central government that the Bakonzo were demanding for a separate district dispels claims and accusations that Isaya Mukirane had declared independence for the Rwenzuru as a "state". It was a mere declaration of independence from the Toro Kingdom and a demand for a separate district in which services could be equitably distributed to serve the entire population.

It had been common practice that under the Toro Kingdom government, the Bakonzo and Bamba were side lined, denied any possible employment in the Omukama's government and bursaries for Education were not extended to people who came from the Rwenzururu dominated areas. A commission of inquiry appointed by the Governor General led by Dr. Sembeguya found out that the Omukama's government in Toro had instituted discrimination and bias as a matter of policy. The Sembeguya report had recommended that "at the general election, Toro should not prevent anybody who was truly representative from standing for elections". It further recommended "present leaders of the rwenzururu must be permitted to return to Toro and stand for election". However, this was not acceptable to the Toro leadership because the Batoro had a tendency of treating Bakonzo and Bamba as inferior and less than human beings. The Sembeguya commission was told of the abusive and arrogant behavior directed by the Batoro to the Bamba and Bakonzo in which Batoro officials called us "apes, gorillas, baboons, dogs, insects, flies and pigs". This was the underlying evidence to confirm why the Batoro refused to include the names of Bamba and Bakonzo in the Toro agreement. The commission urged the Toro government to announce publicly that the three main tribes in the kingdom were Batoro, Bamba and Bakonzo, but the Omukama's government blatantly refused to heed this recommendation, fueling more troubles among the opposing tribes. When the Toro government admitted that the Bamba and Bakonzo areas were **educationally under developed**, the commission recommended "that special arrangements should be made to eliminate the disparity". The report recommended that for five years, funds supplied for bursaries be devoted to the Bamba and Bakonzo students in order to alleviate the disparity in Education. This however, because of discrimination

11

and bias, was never implemented and the Rwenzori area remained behind in all sectors of development. With all these in mind, the movement's rebellion spread all over the Rwenzuru area and attracted more sympathies than condemnation.

In all this the central government was ambivalent about the whole scenario. The Parliament in Kampala while debating the introduction of a state of emergency in the Rwenzuru area, had the guts to listen to members of the Democratic Party who formed the opposition, that the Bakonzo and Bamba be moved by the army to another area so that their homeland may be declared into a National Park. This proposal was put on the floor of parliament by DP Member of Parliament, the Hon. F. Kangwamu from Ankole South-East constituency. Thanks to UPC Minister Hon. Flex Onama who said, "there is no DP, UPC, Protestant, Catholic, in the minds of Bamba and Bakonzo, only Rwenzururu". He was echoing what one of the leaders Mr. Kawamara had said earlier in his statement to the government that, "nothing can be gained by ordering the Uganda Rifles to arrest anybody they simply suspect of being Rwenzururu supporter; everyone who lived in those counties was regarded as a rwenzururian, whether he believes in it or not". It is inconceivable to believe that the Bakonzo and Bamba could still vote the Democratic Party leadership despite the motion moved by a DP member of parliament to have the entire tribe moved and their God given land declared national park for animals. In spite of this, it was an uphill task for the Uganda Peoples' congress to penetrate their campaign in the Ruwenzori. This in part was because at the time the political parties were run based on religions. The fact that the majority of the inhabitants were Catholics; it was a foregone conclusion that they would support the democratic party regardless of what DP members said about us in parliament. This goes as well, to explain why they have gone to vote for politically disoriented people with less developmental ideas as long as they are Catholics.

CHAPTER 3

While the bickering about the security situation in the Rwenzori was going on in parliament, the movement was getting entrenched among all the inhabitants of the mountains of the moon. The army was continuing to arrest and torture persons they suspected of supporting the movement. Houses were being torched and school and health centers were getting deserted since most employees were Batoro and were no longer welcome to work under the movement government. A tax policy had been introduced and Isaya Mukirane's government was now functional both in principle and in practice. Those who refused to subscribe by paying the 'nzururu' tax had to leave the area. Some people opted to pay two taxes, that of the Omukama for fear of retribution by the Uganda army and that of Isaya Mukirane's government for fear of blame by the rest of the Bakonzo who were paying willingly. Despite non-compliance by the Bakonzo for the central government's laws and orders, one of theirs Mr. Timothy Bazarabusa was nominated to represent the Bakonzo in the legislative Council, the *"Legico"* as a back bencher.

During the general election of 1961 DP candidate, Ezironi Bwambale, defeated Mr.Bazarabusa. However, because Bazarabusa was an effective member of the Legico and personally know to the Prime Minister, Dr. Apollo Milton Obote, he was appointed Uganda's first High Commissioner to Britain. This would have been considered a great honor that Obote gave to the Bakonzo, to pick one of theirs to occupy that high office despite the tribal war that was raging on. Dr Obote clearly knew that the Bakonzo did not support his party because they refused to vote for Bazarabusa. By voting for Bwambale of the DP, the Bakonzo were sending a clear message that they would not support the government of Prime Minister Milton Obote. However, Obote did not buy into this; he went an extra mile and appointed a Mukonzo to what was considered the highest office in the foreign affairs ministry.

WHO IS THIS TIMOTHY BAZARABUSA?

Bazarabusa was the son of one mukonzo [munyangetse] called Byabasakuzi. Byabasakuzi and his wife were among some of the first Bakonzo families who were taken to Kabarole as slaves to the Omukama. Timothy Bazarabusa then grew up at the palace and benefited from the palace education facilitation. As a man, he settled in Kasisi, a village near the royal palace. He then married a lady from the Babito clan, the royal clan. This 'Mubitokati' lady gave birth to two girls before she died at an early age. Bazarabusa, then widowed, married a Muganda lady, daughter of Kulubya, the first African Mayor of Kampala.

Bazarabusa did not forget where his family had come from. He used his office as Native.Anglican Church schools supervisor to advocate for building schools in his homeland. While he was working hard to advocate for education in his home area, he was nominated to the "Legico", the Legislative Council as backbencher representating Toro Kingdom.

Prime Minister Apollo Milton Obote later appointed him as the first Uganda High Commissioner to the United Kingdom. The appointment to this office did not please the Omukama's government and was received with impunity by the Batoro loyalists. It remained the highest political appointment the Bakonzo and Bamba had ever received and remained so until 1986 when a full cabinet minister was appointed from those tribes.

Bazarabusa, came home the following year, 1965 to join his government in celebrations of Independence and was found dead in his car, a Volkswagen, that had been driven under a bus. The engine of this car is usually behind and it is said that it was still running while the front was stuck underneath the bus. Whether this was the work of *'Batoro bad elements'* in Kampala or just an accident, has never been known to date, and will probably never be known. There was no inquiry into this death, and it appears there will never be.

CHAPTER 4

Bazarabusa, as schools supervisor in the Omukama's government used this office to build schools in the mountain areas of the Rwenzori. Some of the schools he helped set up that are still standing today include Nyamisule, Nkangi Mahango, Bukangama, Kabingo, and Ihandiro primary Schools. Most of these schools were built with corrugated iron sheets. The enrolment in these schools was very high but the graduates from them did not receive bursaries and/or scholarships from the Toro government as mentioned earlier. When the army moved into the mountain areas hunting for Isaya Mukirane, the schools closed. Most of the teachers fled the areas for fear of revenge because majority of them were Batoro.

In spite of all this backwardness and under development, the people of the Rwenzori remained resilient with a strong hope that one-day favor will come their way. It was not easy at this point to destroy their cause.

In 1963 when I was in grade school, Mr. Bazarabusa came to our school, Kyarumba primary school. He was on a tour to bide the Bakonzo farewell for he was going to take up a senior job as Uganda's High Commissioner to UK. We sang songs for him and while on parade, he asked my headmaster, Mr. Bahindi, a mutoro at that time to allow him to inspect the students. When he came to my line he spotted me, and said to me, " You are a very smart, well dressed boy. How old are you?" When I told him I was 8 years of age, he smiled and reached into his pocket and gave me twenty five cents. I have never forgotten this moment. This was the first time I ever saw him and was also the last. The people of the Rwenzori will never forget the contribution he made towards the development of education in this area. The sprouting of education in this region makes me echo the biblical passage in 1 Corinthians 3:6 which reads, "**I sowed the seed, Apollos watered the plant, but it was God who made the plant grow. The one who sows and the one who waters really do not matter. It is God who matters, because he makes the plant grow.**" This is exactly what had sustained the hopes and aspirations of the Bakonzo and Bamba in achieving their education goals. This biblical analogy strengthened the hopes and faith of the people and as they see those buildings still standing, they surely will take time to forget the promotion of education Bazarabusa initiated. The schools he helped build in his bid to promote education are like a seed he planted, and the 25cents he gave me is the equivalent of a bucket of water he gave me to water the seed. I did not know that 20 years down the road I would jump into Bazarabusa's shoes to advocate for the building of more schools at all levels in order to boost our educational capacity, as I will discuss in later chapters.

As the youngest Member of Parliament ever elected in Uganda, at 26 years of age, I did not have much on my political manifesto, except to recognize that my people were educationally backward, and that the best way forward was to advocate and promote education above all issues. My primary task was to convince the population that education was the best weapon to fight backwardness, poverty, repression and enslavement. At the time Bazarabusa left the scene, backwardness, poverty, and deep frustration dominated the people of the Rwenzori. The people here were the least educated in the Toro Kingdom. The schools Bazarabusa helped to build produced students with brilliant results. But they could not go beyond junior secondary school level. The first junior secondary school which could take graduates from all primary six schools in the entire Rwenzori, was Bwera Junior Secondary school, opened in 1958. Most bright Bakonzo and Bamba were advised to go to teachers' colleges instead of pursuing higher education. Besides, there would be no bursaries for them if they opted to go further. During these early days, it was not possible for anyone to go to Kings College Budo, Namiliango College, St. Mary's Kisubi, Nyakasura, Ntare, Namagunga or Gayaza secondary schools. Mr. Karugaba Selvesta was the first headmaster of Bwera Junior Secondary school in 1958. He was succeeded by Mr. Samwiri Mutoro, the first Rwenzori native to head the highest institution of learning in the Rwenzoris at that time.

Samwiri Mutoro was so innovative that after Karugaba, he initiated a program of Bakonzo and Bamba students looking beyond teacher education and pursuing higher education. He had been a member of the Bakonzo Life History research society started by Isaya Mukirane. He was a famous Mathematics and Religious Knowledge teacher. I remember one of his students who became my primary six teacher, Mr. Uliya Baluku telling us in class that the best way to memorize the names of the North American great lakes as taught by Samuiri Mutoro was by simply saying "**S**amuiri **M**utoro **H**as **E**aten **O**ranges". It is so funny that even in today's North American teaching; they have similar colloquial acronyms for memorizing the famous great lakes. For them in North America they use "**HOMES**" with each letter representing each one of the Great Lakes.

Mr. Samwiri B. Mutooro

Samwiri Mutoro being one of the most highly educated citizens of the Rwenzoris opted to join Politics as a member of the Uganda Peoples Congress and ran for office in 1962. He lost to the Democratic Party candidate, Mr. Ezron Bwambale. The UPC party fielded two candidates at the time while the DP had one candidate. In fact both Samwiri and

Bazarabusa were very valuable candidates. But Dr. Obote chose to have Bazarabusa. Mr. Mutoro opted to go to North America to study Theology in a Montreal Christian college. He died by motor accident on the way to Fort Portal after returning from Canada. During the short period Mutoro was a way from Bwera Junior Secondary School, another dynamic Mukonzo, who later became a Music scholar; Semu AbwoliKiyonga briefly headed the school until 1966. At this time the junior secondary schools were abolished by legislation. Mr. Blasio Maate took over the school as it became a primary school, still regarded as the best in the Rwenzoris, producing candidates to join Secondary Schools. This time with more focus on higher education and no longer teacher education as was the case during the Karugaba years. Some schools in Toro which were Junior Schools were phased out and automatically became secondary schools, but the Ruwenzori ones only became primary schools. Was this pre-planned not to have secondary schools as junior schools were being phased out? This could be partly attributed to weak representation in parliament at the time legislation was introduced to abolish junior secondary schools. With effective representation Rwenzori would have had two secondary schools by promoting Bwera and Nsenyi junior schools to secondary. They were however both demoted to primary schools.

Following the Sembeguya Commission Report, government had set up a desk in the office of the District Education Officer to oversee the schools in Bwamba and Busongora. The first person in charge of this desk was one Mr. Nantamu all the way from Busoga. By this time the Native Anglican Church had surrendered the administration of schools to the government as the UPC sought to end the relationship between religion and politics. Nantamu tried his best to improve on the existing schools. His work was complicated by the on going war between the Batoro and Isaya Mukirane's rebel militia. After Nantamu, we had Rwatsika and later Rucecerwa; all serving as Education officers, and very little is known about their major contributions towards education in the area other than purely administrative. What I remember about them especially Mr. Ruchecherwa was for him to visit schools that wanted an extension of a classroom. Whenever a school wanted to move on to the next grade, the education officer or the inspector of schools as they were called at that time came to see whether the school should have an additional class. In most cases they looked at the enrolment and the potential for expansion. Pupils were called to parade. The education official inspected the parade by walking along each line which represented each class. This was the best way they could ascertain the number of pupils per class;carrying out a head count. They did not want to go by the register, because sometimes some pupils were not registered either because they did not pay fees or simply had just absconded after the registration. A physical head count on the parade was the best way to know the school enrolment. The other reason why they insisted on parade was because most of the teachers and head teachers at the time were not qualified. The qualified Batoro had left due to the insurgency and the schools were left to be manned by untrained people. The pupils were ill trained below accepted standards for many years. For example in English most teachers were as 'green' as the pupils they taught. For example during school band performance which happened on every market day, the whole school with teachers alike could go on singing a song in what sounded like English for many years without knowing what the actual pronunciations of the words were and even the meaning of the song. Here is a typical example of one common song which was sung by most if not all the schools in the school band: "**oh John wazeverio.ooh oooh John wazaveria- . John friend mayi**" This was sang by many students and even as late as July 2006 one such former student in those schools now living in the United States did not know what that song was except to continue telling his children that they used to sing "oh john wazeverio…" during parades and school bands. When I actually told that father of six children; what the song should have been, he was almost hysterical to see what kind of injustice he went through as he struggled to earn his education. The song actually was: "oh John was a warrior, ooh oooh John was warrior; John French man." The intention of the song was to teach the pupils to match like John who was a warrior and a French man in the Second World War. School bands instilled discipline among pupils. That is why the education systems allowed it in their school curriculum.

Dr. Apollo Milton Obote, MP

Now came the general elections of 1962 and the politicians of both the Democratic Party and the Uganda Peoples Congress were scrambling about trying to cajole the people into voting for them. At this time, the Uganda People's Congress fielded Mr. Samuiri Mutooro, a teacher and an educational reformer. This was a man who would have taken over

Bazarabusa's job even more effectively. He however, lost the election to Mr. Bwambale a second time. Again the DP candidate prevailed. These two elections of 1961 and 1962 signified that UPC was unpopular among the Bakonzo and Bamba. This was greatly due to the fact that Prime Minister Obote, who was the leader of the UPC, did not grant the request Isaya had put across, which was, separation from the Toro Kingdom. The issue of separate districts had been discussed in the Legislative council and the motion had been defeated. Of course, Prime Minister Obote could not unliterary order for the creation of separate districts, when parliament had voted no. He was strictly observing the principle of ruling by consensus. Prime Minister Obote believed in parliamentary democracy and could not become dictatorial just for the sake of the Bamba and Bakonzo. This however, was not appreciated by Isaya's movement, the struggle continued and this time more tension mounted in all over the Rwenzoris. Dr. Obote had the intellectual stimulation of dealing with difficult political issues, but he was dealing with a national assembly that had a member of the opposition representing the disturbed area. I believe he missed the despondency of not being able to come up with answers, which gave him very little emotional reward. The people in the Rwenzoris would have loved to see Dr. Obote act unliterary against the Batoro and this would have opened a window for any UPC candidate to win in an election in the Rwenzururu areas. The people in the Rwenzoris voted for the Democratic Party of Ben Kiwanuka. This is the only time they were able to side with the Omukama's government by voting alongside their traditional foes.

CHAPTER 5

The whole of 1963 saw the Rwenzuru rebellion intensified and the entire mountain range was on fire. The army had moved in and camped on mountain tops because they feared rolling stones; one of the weapons of the bakonzo fighters. Stone rolling had been proved effective in the Bwamba region and was being used in the Bukonzo and Busongora areas as well.

The Uganda Argus of February 21, 1963 reported that "One police constable was hit on the face by rolling stones and received stitches". This happened when police went to investigate an incident in Bwamba village. A mob of Bamba people attacked the police with rolling stones and got away with it. This kind of insecurity became rampant in the rest of the mountain area. Public and essential services came to a stand still. School and health centers closed. All injuries were taken either to Kabarole hospital or Kilembe mines hospital.

My headmaster, Mr. Bahindi had been attacked by a mob of Rwenzuru soldiers and had fled to Toro... never to return. A caretaker headmaster was appointed to head the Kyarumba primary school. This was now the only school that was open. It only run up to primary six. Graduates from this school had to travel all the way to Bwera to join the junior school, others traveled to Nsenyi Junior Secondary. These were the only highest institution of learning in the Kasese and Bundibugyo districts for a long time. At least during the disturbances, one school in each sub county remained open. Most of these schools had to be on the lower lands in order for them to receive protection from the central government. The Toro government was not bothered about the closures of schools because their own schools were running. When Batoro teachers left our areas, they were quickly deployed to teach in schools in other parts of the Toro kingdom. In 1964, while we were in class, an attempt was made to close our school too. A group of 6 Rwenzuru soldiers armed with sticks descended on the school. They surrounded the small building that housed class five and six. Mr. Yofesi Tembo was acting headmaster and also teaching in the grade five classroom. He was dragged out of the class, beaten with sticks across his chest and across his back before his students. These six revolutionary young fighters besieged the class. We were in the lower building of the school and when we saw what it had happened, we jumped through the windows and fled for our lives. The teachers too in these buildings fled instead of coming to the aid of their colleague. Mr. Tembo with a bunch of other grade two teachers was about the highest qualified personnel in the Bukonzo and Bwamba counties. They were determined to keep the schools in the region opened. We did not have grade three teachers at this time. While most of the resources for development came from the Bukonzo area like the taxes from the Katwe salt lake, the taxes from the Kilembe mines, the sale of coffee and cotton, taxes from the tourist industry attracted by Queen Elizabeth National Park to name but a few; The authorities in fort Portal did not mind about developing the region from where they received most of their revenue in taxes. Most development took place in the Toro area. During the colonial time under the Omukama's government, schools were built to cater for the entire Toro Kingdom, but all of them were built in Toro, a simple sign that Rwenzori was just not considered part of the Toro Kingdom; this being one of the factors that made Isaya intensify his rebellion. Nyakasura one of the oldest schools in Uganda was built in the Toro area, Butiti teachers college, Canon Apollo teachers college, Kicwamba technical college, St. Leos College Kyegobe, Mpaga high school, Kyebambe girls' secondary school. These educational institutions were all concentrated in one area, with approximately 10 kilometers from each other. And to make matters worse, for a Mukonzo to be admitted in these institutions, you either had to change your name and sound like you are a Mutoro, or you had to completely change your personality and become a Mutoro. This irregularity in the education sector went on almost until 1980. People used to hide their personalities and pretend to belong to either a certain clan or tribe that was associated with the powers that was. A lot of our brilliant people who had passed very highly after their junior secondary school from Bwera and Nsenyi could not be admitted to these institutions. The lucky ones ended up going to Kakoba Teachers college, and a few who managed to beat the system ended up going to Kampala's day schools or Private Schools. Bakonzo and Bamba students who had names that sounded like Byabasaija, Tibaijuka, Bagarukayo, Kobusinge, Katuramum, Byabagambe, Kobujune, Byaruhanga, Mbabazi, Baguma etc found favor with the Toro education authority. Imagine and compare the two junior schools we had in Kasese and none in Bwamba to the many I mentioned earlier situated in Fort Portal. It was unbelievable that in spite of all the education injustice, we had a small group of elite who managed to educate the generation that followed. The issue of scholarships and bursaries was unheard of when it came to students from Kasese and Bwamba. One of the earliest graduates from Bukonzo is Dr. Barnabas Rwatooro [RIP] Does his name of Rwatoro ring any bells? He was the first Mukonzo to graduate from Makerere University with a medical degree in 1967. Since independence in 1962, up till 1967, Toro Kingdom already had several graduates, while the Banyarwenzuru saw their first only in 1967.

The first female graduate was Bonabana Kitakakire Candida in 1972 from Makerere University, Kampala. Does her name of Bonabana ring any bells? She got a Bachelor of Social Work and Social Administration [SWASA]. She went to Nsenyi Primary, Mary Hill in Mbarara and Trinity College Nabbingo. But if you consider the rest of the Toro Kingdom, lots of graduated in various field were in abundance even as early as 1960 before Uganda earned her

25

independence. Between 1960 and 1967 there were zero graduate in the Bakonzo and Bamba areas.

In the department of Agriculture, we did not have a qualified agriculture officer to advise our peasants on agricultural methods. The highest qualified agricultural officer was Mr. Paul Nzobindo in 1968 with just a diploma in agriculture. The Bukonzo area was one of the highest producers of Maize, coffee, cotton and other substance crops. But our people just used their own crude method of farming to produce for a living. Our students who would have gone to school to specialize in Agriculture were not given the motivation and encouragement from the Toro Education authority. Most of our young men and girls were encouraged to take up teaching at grade two level; although these were just the lucky ones. The Bukonzo and Busongora counties were famous for the production of copper and salt. Both of these commodities earned plenty of revenue in taxes to the Toro government, but there were no kickbacks injected in the Bakonzo economy. All the wealthy were concentrated in the Kabarole areas to develop the Omukama's "favorite territory". Busongora County was famous for the production of fish and a booming industry was placed on Lake George, at Kasenyi called "The Uganda Fish Marketing African Corporation" [TUFMAC]. You could not find a qualified Mukonzo or Mwamba working in this fishing industry. Our people only provided casual and manual labor. Most of them were termed group employees. This merely meant that we provided unskilled labor. Why, because we were not educated enough to sit in comfortable positions within the fish plant. . But there were Batoro and other 'gentlemen' from other tribes who were well educated, some of them as fisheries officers with degrees, diplomas and certificates working in and around the lakes in the Bakonzo land. Some people often argue that Ugandans are free to work anywhere as long as there was work. But the point I am making here is that even at a local level at Kasenyi, we could not find a native from the Bakonzo land who had even a certificate to be able to work along with other Ugandans. Besides, we did not have any Mukonzo or Mwamba working else where in Uganda, if we have to argue that Ugandans are free to work anywhere as long as there is work and are qualified to do so. This brought imbalance in opinion generating especially when it came to the location of resources for development. It was ironical that even with the factory on Lake George, at Kasenyi, a decent primary school was never constructed to cater for the surrounding population. Little wonder, everybody who worked here did not have their families here, so they could not have feelings for the people who were providing them with local manpower and food; by thinking and working towards putting up a decent school for the kids. They had no kids of their own to go into the school because better schools were already in place where they hailed from. If they ever did, however, it would not please the Omukama of Toro because, then the local people would go to this school, get an education and have their eyes open to see the injustice that was going on within the Kingdom leadership. The omukama feared educated challenge. If you take the example of Kilembe Mines; copper was being mined from the ground, under people's homes. There was no notice ever given to indigenous people that pipes will be passing under their homes or hills, there by proposing what could have been a financial benefit from the industry. Schools were build by the mine authorities especially so because the management was by Canadian expatriates who were obligated to build schools for their children. The kids of the natives were not allowed in these schools unless their parents worked in the mines. What is funny here is that even the manual laborers who worked underground the mines came from as far as Kabale and Kabarole. One can argue that maybe the Bakonzo were unwilling to work in the mines. But this is not true. What is true is that with very little education it was general knowledge that they can not fit in the work force where the administrative structures were managed by foreigners. The Batoro and Bakiga fitted in because they had some basic education and their children benefited by attending these mine school. However in spite of all these, Isaya Mukirane and his team had seen all the injustice and were busy calling upon all the Bakonzo and Bamba to follow and support the demand for a separate kingdom in order that the Bakonzo might be able to administer their own resources. Isaya had marshaled up the support of a large number of peasants who formed the majority of the population. The middle class, if there was any at this time, was a little ambivalent about the ambitions of the proclaimed "king", although their fears were put to rest as the struggle progressed. As the fighting raged on, so was the hatred between the Bakonzo and the Batoro. Skirmishes between these groups of people continued on both the Bwamba side and the Bukonzo/Busongora side of the Omukama' Kingdom. One of the issues I believe Prime Minister Milton Obote did not want to consider was the creation of another Kingdom, because he was already planning to get rid of Kingdoms and declare Uganda a Republic. In 1966 the Uganda Peoples Congress, UPC came up with the republican constitution in which all Kingdoms were to be dissolved or were they to be abolished? In 1967 Dr. Obote became the President of Uganda and dropped the post of Prime Minister. There were changes in the central government; however these did not affect the Rwenzuru Kingdom. Isaya Mukirane had insisted earlier that his kingdom could not be abolished together with the rest of the Kingdoms because; in the first place it was not recognized under the 1962 independence constitution. "We neither had a kingdom or a district. This Kingdom was self-proclaimed and self-independent by June 30, 1962". Isaya Mukirane together with the people who lived around the Rwenzoris and supported him had constituted themselves into "an independent kingdom" opposed to the Toro Kingdom and sought from the central government to separate from the Toro Kingdom. Both the demands for a Kingdom or a district had been denied by the powers that were. This is exactly why the war of the Rwenzururu did not end. The entire tribes of the Bakonzo, Basongora, Banyabindi, Bamba, Batuku and Babulebule, were dissatisfied with the leadership at the time and unanimously agreed to continue to fight until separation was achieved. The only umbrella under which they could all fit while fighting for their human rights was the "Rwenzuru umbrella" under the leadership of "king" Isaya Mukirane. Some people have even up to today interpreted the declaration of independence by Isaya as declaration of state sovereignty. Historian Dr. Arthur Syahuka-Muhindo, in The Rwenzururu Movement and the Democratic Struggle says; *"in general terms, this attitude which was initiated by Kaboyo as the founder of the Toro State caused class misalignment right from the start of the Kingdom. Dominant local classes were subordinated to largely alien ones in the power structure of Toro Kingdom. This encouraged more Balisa, Basita, and Bahinda clans to migrate to Toro to consolidate and benefit from Babito rule there. The political consequence of this process was the erosion of power and freedom for the Baamba and Bakonzo as a people. ...The Toro establishment was resisted by local dominant classes because of the nature of its organization and its political orientation. The chiefs of Busongora and Bukonzo vehemently resisted the new rule."*[p284].

As Prof. Muhindo further contends, "kingdoms or settlements south of Lake George were generally referred to as States." It was therefore a misconstrued idea to refer to the Rwenzururu Kingdom as a sovereign state. This was not Isaya's intention because even Isaya's close associates like Mupalya and Kwamara who on many occasions led delegations to meet with the central government leadership, talked of separate district and not 'state'. Although politicians from opposing opinions floated ideas that Rwenzuru was created to establish an Rwenzururu state; records will show that this is not true. The Bakonzo/Bamba intended to secede from Toro Kingdom as it were. In the document signed by Isaya, Kawamara and Mupalya during the declaration of Independence in June 1962, the trio after reiterating the grievances for the Bamba/Bakonzo against Batoro closed their document by saying;

*"Now let us all be in wait, no brutality, nor torture shall make us ever plead for mercy, for we prefer peace and freedom of speech in an **independent Uganda** to malicious Batoro Government. Long live Uganda.* Uhuru!" [p298]

Historians have recorded that "when the Bakonzo/Bamba leaders learned that the Toro Constitutional Committee members were going to leave for Entebbe without their representatives, they decided to send a Bakonzo Bamba party too. ... It was at this dramatic meeting with the Governor on February 26 1962 that Mukirane, as the leader of the Bamba/Bakonzo delegation handed to him the memorandum which demanded a separate district for the Bamba/Bakonzo.[p296] It is therefore, inconceivable for any sober minded leader to think of statehood around the Ruwenzori's when the original leaders did not conceive that idea of statehood. Mukirane made several attempts to send delegations to OAU and the United Nations, but failed constantly. He wanted the plight of the Bakonzo and Bamba to be heard by higher authorities, those that would sympathize with our human right situation and put pressure on the central government to listen to the rwenzururu grievances. Isaya Mukirane continued with his vision to liberate the Bakonzo and Bamba from the tyranny inflicted upon them by their oppressors, the Omukama's Batoro people. Isaya was a mere Grade two teacher who was not even accorded the privilege of being a headmaster of a primary school. He had only been elected to represent the Bakonzo Bamba in the Toro parliament out of which he walked when the Toro parliament refused a resolution to include the Bakonzo and Bamba and the Lukonzo and Rwamba languages in the Toro Agreement. The Toro parliament had succeeded in making sure that the Bakonzo/Bamba do not receive recognition as part of Ugandan society. Isaya together with other movement leaders also challenged the motion put forward by Samson Rusoke, the last Omuhikirwa [Prime Minister] of the Toro Kingdom, which declared that "only a Mutoro Nyakabara shall be Katikiro of Toro" in 1962. According to Dr. Arthur Syahuka Muhindo, "a mutooro Nyakabara means 'a proper or Real Mutoro – that one whose origin is Babito' p284. This notion was discriminatory and was meant to eliminate any Mukonzo or Mwamba who would aspire to become Katikiro. Such qualities had been seen in Isaya and other bakonzo leaders like Timothy Bazarabusa and Yeremiya Kawamara. To the Omukama's parliament, all Bakonzo were to be considered Batoro and there would be no language called Lukonzo, this therefore would give room for anybody to aspire for the powerful post of Katikiro. The Batoro were further intimidated by the qualities they had seen in the Rwenzururu leaders that they made sure that they remained in jail during the National Parliamentary elections which would have probably returned them to a National parliament, where they could have aired their view to a more understanding forum. Because the Bakonzo and Bamba lacked representation in the Omukama's government, when it came to development, and distribution of services, priority was given to the Batoro, and if anything remained on the budget; then it would spill over to the Rwenzoris. To Isaya and his colleagues, who included Mr. Bulasio Maate, this was ridiculous and had to be resisted by force even if it meant the entire tribe perishing. One other factor which infuriated the Bakonzo and Bamba according to Authur Syahuka-Muhindo was the fact that Isaya, Kawamara and Mupalya were quickly jailed at the time they would be contesting for elections to go to the legislative council to voice the grievances of their people against the Batoro. The three leaders were quickly tried in a Kangaroo type of court on the eve of the London Conference of June 1962. The Bakonzo leaders wrote a letter to the central government and gave copies to the governor and the colonial secretary, complaining about the actions of the judges who passed judgment against their three leaders so that they could be left in prison while Batooro leaders went to the Conference to ask for federal status. The Bakonzo /Bamba leaders while on trial expected an acquittal since they did not have any case to answer, and were well preparing to travel to London to attend the Constitutional Conference. Instead the Batooro judges paved their way to jail.

Isaya Mukirane did not live long to see the fruits of his resistance. He fell sick with typhoid fever and died on 2nd September 1966. He was buried on Bulemba Hill in Ihandiro. A public moaning was held all over the mountain areas covering the present Kasese and Bundibugyo Districts. Isaya was moaned in the counties of Burahya, Bunyangabo, Busongora, Bakonzo, and Bwamba.

CHAPTER 6

Isaya Mukirane 1964

During this time all the primary schools on the lower lands of the Rwenzori were closed. Those on the mountain areas remained open but with no teachers. The rwenzururu leadership hired teachers of all kinds, most of them were grade level, and most had not studied beyond class four. I remember one of the schools I went to at

Katabona primary school had classes up to grade four and the headmaster who was also the grade four teacher, was a grade four graduate. My father did not want me to be taught in primary four by a teacher who was also a primary four graduate. He moved me to Butale School where we were 4 children in a class and the teacher there too was just a grade five graduate. Most of the schools managed and administered by the 'kingdom' leadership had ill trained personnel let alone the buildings in which they were operating. When the "king" died, in 1966, his son Charles Wesley Mumbere was barely turning 15 years and was in the kind of school like I have described above. He was not allowed to become 'king' immediately since he was under age. A team of elders surrounded him and managed the affairs of the movement until he turned 18 when he was fully coroneted as king of the Bakonzo and Bamba, in the rwenzururu movement style. Charles Wesley had special teachers who went to the Buhikira Royal Palace to tutor him. One of these teachers was Mr. Christopher Tembo Kabwemi. He was not a qualified teacher, but since all it took was one to know some basic English and basic mathematics, he passed on some elementary teaching to the 'king'. All this was because our people did not have qualified trained manpower, a basic service that was systematically denied us by our colonizers. The generation that went to school during this period had either to be sent to the lower lands for schooling or continued in ill equipped schools without qualified teachers and just hopped for the best. I was one of those who stayed up with the rwenzururu schools. My father was one of the 'rebels' who could not betray the movement by sending me to the lower land schools. By sending ones children in the lower land schools meant that you became an accomplice, a hypocrite and were betraying the very movement that was fighting for your equality. These schools were managed by the Toro government and were subject to frequent attacks from the movement soldiers. By this time they were heavily armed with spears and knives, no longer sticks and clubs. After Isaya had died, the movement was divided and the people were also divided. Those who become disillusioned by the continuous fighting moved and decided to live in protected camps on the lower lands where the Uganda rifles could offer protection. They were put in camps referred to as "internal displaced people". They were locally known as "bakolikoli" meaning betrayers. The rwenzururu leaders had a general name for them as "esyandaghangali", which meant those who have betrayed the cause of the movement by siding with the central government. They then started helping the Uganda rifles in hunting down the die-hard Rwenzururu who chose to remain on the high lands. At this time the movement had put a mechanism in place to collect graduated tax from all those who cherished and supported the cause of the movement. They now operated a government equivalent to the Toro Kingdom one. They had appointed ministers, chiefs and local leaders. The movement continued to collect graduated taxes from those faithful ones and agents who were living amongst them for spying purposes collected even some taxes from among the 'bakolikoli' privately. In October of 1966 the lowland group, for refusing to bring me to a legitimate school arrested my father. He would only be released if he agreed to bring me to Kyarumba primary school. My father had no choice but to comply. That October, I came in the middle of third term to complete my grade four class. I was lucky they promoted 15 students out of a total of 16 students. Had I not been among the 15 students, I would have been forced to repeat the class. At this time my headmaster, a qualified teacher was Mr. Yosia Muhindo, famously known as Kireru. He was my English teacher and was considered at the time as the best English teacher in the whole Kasese region. He was later nominated to go for a short course in English at the University of Makerere. He was the only headmaster who was chosen by the Omukama's government, to go for this prestigious course. As a result he became well know by the Education authorities in the Toro district and was later transferred to head a more populated school, Karambi which was on the lower land and controlled by the bakolikoli group. Mr. Muhindo became one of the best interpreters from English to Lukonzo for any foreign guest who visited the rwenzori region. This famous teacher although full of intellect, did not advance beyond head teacher at grade two level; not because he did not have school fees, but the Tooro education authorities would not let him. He too was a victim of discrimination. He later retired in the 80s and became the district executive secretary, a post he held until 1985. When he left Kyarumba in 1967, another dynamic headmaster, Mr. Nyamayaro Ezra was appointed to take his place. He initiated the rebuilding of the school since it was on the brink of collapse. The Toro government's Education authority had neglected most schools in "disturbed" areas of the Ruwenzori's. Kyarumba primary school was among the many schools, which did not receive any attention since the uprising of the movement. It was considered hidden in the cupboard. Mr. Nyamayaro who hails from the Kiyonga family mobilized the parents of Kyarumba School to collect money instead of depending on the Education authority to provide funding. They would then put up a permanent block of buildings. A permanent foundation was started but got stack and could not take off from the foundation due to lack of extra funding from the government to reinforce what the parents provided. By l968 the building block had not taken off. Later Ezra was transferred leaving his project unfinished. This was the first time I ever saw a head teacher of a primary school organizing a fundraising without government help. Mr. Nyamayaro set the example for building a school on self help and many schools were to follow. Kyarumba Primary School was one of the few schools that were upgraded to grade seven levels when the central government abolished the junior school system in 1966. However, grade seven did not come until 1969. The first bunch of students to sit grade seven from this school traveled seven miles to Kisinga to sit for their primary leaving exam. I was one of the first candidates to sit grade seven at Kyarumba in 1969. Grade six graduates from this school either went to Bwera Junior School, Nsenyi junior school, or just disappeared amongst the population and started teaching in the mountain schools. Most of the manpower for the counties of Busongora and Bwamba was generated from the two junior schools we had at that time, i.e. Bwera junior secondary and Nsenyi junior secondary schools. These two were established on religious foundations to cater for the two prominent religions in the area, a system that was divisive, designed by the omukama's government to divide and rule the Bamba and Bakonzo. Most of the

35

graduates from these two junior secondary schools ended up in teachers' collages, not by choice but by council. That is Butiti Teachers' College accepted those from Nsenyi while Canon Apollo College accepted those from Bwera. Very few managed to go to senior secondary school. 1967 was the last year we saw junior secondary schools. Government introduced legislation to abolish junior schools and have primary level go from one to seven and senior was to go from nine to twelve, while high school was to go from thirteen to fourteen. As grade seven was introduced in several schools, educational materials did not reach all the schools. Many of the schools that were accorded the status of primary seven did not even have the buildings to house their grade seven students. Some hosted them under trees and others used nearby churches to accommodate this extra class. When time for examination came, the candidates for grade seven were collected at centers where exams could be distributed. In 1968 the candidates for grade seven leaving exams from Kyarumba were asked to travel to Kisinga on foot to go and sit for the exam. At this time there was only one primary school, Kyarumba that was accorded the status of grade seven. Schools like Ngangi, Nyamusule and Mahango, which were introduced and built by the Bazarabusa initiative, could not receive primary seven statuses because they were under the Rwenzururu leadership and their enrolment was very low. Other schools like Kitolu, Kanyatsi, Kyondo and Nyakiyumbu suffered the same fate. Most of these schools had the building structures, but did not have the required enrolment and of course had poorly trained teachers. These however, with their meager enrolment continued to become main contributors of students to fill up the newly introduced grade seven levels. Academic performance here was not exciting mainly because the teachers were not well qualified. Again this was a systematic ploy to keep the Bakonzo under educated for fear of competition with the Batoro. The abolition of junior secondary opened a new era in the education system of the entire country, Uganda. This opened a new way for the Bakonzo and Bamba students to by- pass the Toro leadership and join senior secondary schools in other areas of the country. The bursary allotment however was still centralized in Kabarole and only very few of the Bamba/Bakonzo students gained from the bursary scheme. The parents supported most of the students who were able to go to senior secondary schools. They had to be well to do parents to afford school fees. When they abolished the junior secondary school in 1967, Kisinga sub-county was seeing their first graduate from Makerere University, the late Dr. Baranaba Rwatooro. Interestingly enough, he went to Kisinga primary school, then Bwera Primary School and later to Kabarole Junior Secondary School. He then went to Nyakasura Secondary school before joining Makerere University. **He was the first Mukonzo to obtain a degree.** Remember his name was "Rwatoro".

By Uganda's independence time in 1962, there were no graduates in Bwamba and Bukonzo/Busongora. The highest educated person in Bwamba was Yositasi Nzenze Bwambale. Together with Timothy Bazarabusa, they were the most highly educated personalities the Rwenzoris could offer to the central government at independence. This partly accounts for why Dr. Obote appointed Timothy Uganda's High Commission to United Kingdom. Very little is known of what became of Mr. Nzenze. The first Muyira from Bwera to graduate was the Late Amon Bazira. He too was product of Bwera Junior Secondary School and Nyakasura High School before he went to Makerere where he graduated in 1970. Busongora did not see their first graduate until 1980 in the name of **Jorome Mbura Muhindo**.

He went to Katiri Primary School in Kilembe and St. Mary's Kisubi before he went to Makerere University. So do you ever wonder why we did not have as many Bakonzo/Bamba boys and girls going through this Kilembe Mines School? The reason is simple. At this time the labor force at Kilembe was dominated by Batooro and Bakiga, which meant that only their kids went to the mine schools. Mbura Muhindo is only one of the very few who went to a mine school and actually made to University.

Jerome Mbura Muhindo went to Katiri Primary school, passed his grade seven and was admitted to Kisubi secondary school. He later joined Makerere University and graduated in 1980. He became the headmaster of Kasese secondary after losing elections he contested first on a UPM ticket and later crossed into the Democratic party of Paul Kawanga Semogerere. He became the first student of Busongora to graduate from University 1980

By 1971 when the Infamous Gen. Idi Amin took power, Kasese District had barely 6 graduates to account for in the Rwenzori area. One wonders how many could the omukama's kingdom account for when they had Nyakasura, St; Leos Kyegobe, Kyebambe and Mpanga, all fully government funded school spewing their products into Makerere University. I leave this to the reader to guess.

The Bakonzo/Bamba/Basongora did not see their first **female doctor until 1982 in the name of Dr. Florance Kabugho.** [RIP]. She got her degree from Makerere University Kampala. She went to Kitalikibi Primary School, Mundongo Primary school, and Kyebambe Girls School,

Trinity College Nabbingo and Makerere University, Kampala. She got her master's degree in Medicine and past on untimely in 2001.

Education in the Rwenzoris progressed at a slow pace, as there were not many if any institutions of higher learning. The first Doctors of Philosophy PhD was attained in 1977 from Harvard University by Dr. Henry Edward Bwambale [RIP]. Dr. Bwambale, like many academicians from this region went through thick and thin to get this Degree. He is the first graduate to hail from Karambi Sub County. He received a Bachelor of Commerce in 1972, and later that year was able to beat the Amin regime's intelligence, as they were hunting the elite, he flew to Iraq to pursue a Masters Degree and later joined Harvard University in Boston for his Doctor of Philosophy Degree. I will discuss Dr. Bwambale's political contributions in a later chapter.

Below now find a break down of graduates by Subcounty. Only 32 had graduated by 1980.

Table 1: Graduates by Sub county

	Names	*Degree*	*Year*	*County*
1	Dr. Rwatooro Barnabas [RIP]	Ch. B, M. B	1967	Kisinga
2	Police - Apuuli Stephen [RIP]	B.A.	1968	Munkunyu
3	Kitakakire Bartholomew	B.A.	1969	Kisinga
4	Bazira Amon [RIP]	B.Phil.	1970	Bwera
5	Mukiraine Joseph [RIP]	B.Sc.	1970	Kisinga
6	Kabagambe John[RIP]	B.Com	1970	Katwe
7	Kabagambe Paddy	B.Sc	1971	Karambi
8	Bwambale Henry [RIP]	B.Com.	1972	Karambi

9	Muhindo Enoch Jim Sakalombi	B.Ed	1972	Bwera
10	Bonabana Kitakakire Candida	SWASA	1972	Kisinga
11	Maate Enos	B.Com	1972	Bwera
12	Tibasaga Kitakakire Thereza	B.A. (Ed)	1973	Kisinga
13	Kighoma Eria	B.Com	1973	Munkunyu
14	Masereka Mutiba	B.A (Ed)	1974	Munkunyu
15	Muhindo Victor[RIP]	B.A	1974	Bwera
16	Abwolikiyonga Semu	B.A	1974	Bwera
17	Kabarole Elijah	B. A	1974	Kisinga
18	Biira Hannah [RIP]	B. A (Ed)	1974	Kyarumba
19	Muhindo Mukirane Hannah	B.Sc. (Ed)	1975	Bwera
20	Byalebeka Kamabu John	B.Sc. Agric	1975	Bwera
21	Muhindo Lazaro [RIP]	B.Sc.	1975	Kisinga
22	Katanga Kitakakire John [RIP]	B.Sc. Agric	1975	Kisinga
23	Kambere Selevester	B.Com	1975	Kisinga
24	Bwambale Yostasi	B.Sc	1975	Bwera
25	Bwambale Misaki [RIP]	B.Sc. [Eng.]	1976	Bwera
26	Biira Loice	B.Sc.(Ed)	1977	Bwera
27	Mbayahi Bwambale Jethro	B. Ed	1977	Kisinga
28	Baluku Stephen	B.A.(Ed)	1976	Bwera
29	Kiyonga B. Crispus	Ch.B, M.B	1978	Bwera
30	Nduru Deo [RIP]	B.Com.	1979	Bwera
31	Kahindo David	B.Sc	1979	Bwera
32	Mbura-Muhindo Jerome	B.Sc. Ed	1980	Kilembe

Currently the number of graduates has gotten beyond 450. I will discuss the reasons for this upsurge and the celebration to it in a later chapter, but first let me discuss the political era post Isaya Mukirane. Remember, not until Amin came on the scene, we are still talking of Rwenzururu fighting for a separate kingdom even though 'kingdoms' ceased to exist in Uganda in 1967, when Uganda became a republic.

CHAPTER 7

The Charles Wesley Iremangoma era: Myth or Reality?

Irema Ngoma simply means the "ruler" of the drum. In local dialect, the kingdom is referred to as the Drum, [Engoma the realm]. The Batoro referred to their king as 'Omukama" and the Bakonzo/

Bamba did not want to use the same word since it was a 'Lutooro' meaning for King. The Bakonzo/Bamba came up with their own title according to the requirements of their language and tradition. To be crown king is referred to as to "erisinga" and the person who are being crown is referred to as the 'Omusinga' and the kingdom for which they are being crown is referred to as the 'Obusinga'. Therefore in this context, the Bakonzo/Bamba referred to their Kingdom as the "Obusinga Bwa Rwenzuru" and the man in charge was referred to as the Omusinga. This can also be the substitute for Mr. Before the name. Omusinga Charles Wesley Mumbere, otherwise referred to as Irema Ngoma succeeded his father later than was expected since he was a minor at the time his father died in 1966.

Charles Mumbere, born in 1951 did not become "king" until he was 18 years. A team of elders shielded him while he grew to become of age; they run the affairs of the "obusinga". Regent Minister in the name of Yohana Mwambalaluli headed the elders. In 1969, at a colorful ceremony at Kahinda Ngoma, Kalingwe, Charles was coroneted King of the Bakonzo/Bamba and all other tribes within the Rwenzori. Many people from the lower lands climbed the mountains to attend the ceremony. School children climbed the mountains to perform, and sing for the new King. The elders who were running the kingdom, surrendered power to Charles, and he assumed the responsibilities of the kingdom. He had grown up as Charles Kisembo, which simply meant the "gift" in the local dialect; and when he became king, the name Kisembo was overshadowed and replaced by the title "IremaNgoma". He had been called Kibanzanga 11 after his Father, which meant that the Kingdom will find him if the central government cannot give it to him. However, this changed when Charles became king, because he and the elders asserted that he was no longer waiting for the kingdom to come; it was already there and he was now the 'King'. He had been trained as a solider and he ruled the kingdom as a military king. He had not received formal education, except by special teachers who themselves were not qualified to teach. He used to read newspapers and magazine from overseas sent to him by Tom Stacey, the man who was close to his father and to the Bakonzo as a tribe in general.

Charles was a young and energetic king who trained and drilled with his young soldiers and changed the mode of leadership from the elderly folk's style to a youthful style with lots of young soldiers surrounding him. His training staff included two run away soldiers from the regime of Idi Amin. These were Staff Sergeant Mwagavumbi and Lt. Paul Byakatonda. Paul Byakatonda run away from the Uganda Air force after surviving the Entebbe raid by Israel Camondoes. Idi Amin hunted all soldiers who survived the attack and called them collaborators. Paul and others took off for their lives and he found himself hiding in the mountains. He together with Mwagavumbi trained the king and promoted him to the rank of "rebel general" at Kahindangoma school of "infantry" with a ceremony officiated by his own chief of staff "major" Richard Kinyamusitu. He centralized his leadership, by becoming the head of the Kingdom and the commander in chief of the army while creating the office of the prime minister who was the head of the government. The Prime minister otherwise called the 'omulerembera' chaired cabinet meetings and oversaw the day to day running of the kingdom. The Omusinga Charles was the head of the Privy Council, which was seated by his appointees. This council acted as the advisory committee to the king on matter pertaining to the administration of the kingdom. He chaired the defense council as the Commander in chief of the army. This council comprised of the various commanders and both the minister of defense and that of internal affairs.

When General Amin was sent by Dr. Obote to fight the Rwenzuru under Isaya Mukirane, he confronted them as militia men but when in 1969 Charles assumed leadership, Amin found young men armed not only with spears and sticks, but with guns ranging from SMGs or submachine guns to motors and Rocket Propelled grenades. The youthful Charles came with sophisticated armory and there is a mystery as to where he might have acquired these arms.

One might ask a question as to what happened to the revolution which was lead by the three founder of the resistance; Nyamutswa, Kapoli and Tibamwenda. Indeed what happened is just the suppression of human rights as these three had intended to fight for the rights of the Bayira, before they were hanged and buried in one grave at Kagando. In fact, one of them, Mr. Tibamwenda left behind a wife who was pregnant and later delivered a baby boy and named him Cyril Makoma. In all local organizations, this young Man Cyril Makoma should have succeeded his father and spear-head the revolution, but the colonial masters at the time together with the Batooro, made sure that this revolution does not resurface. Killing the trio and burying them in one grave was meant to scare off any person related to them to ever revive the revolution. Although it was more of a traditional revolution, it was fighting for the human rights of the oppressed Bayira. Even the name Bayira from that time changed to Bakonzo; a derogatory name meaning dogs in the Ruhenda language of Tooro. Later when the white missionaries traveled over the hills of Rwenzori, they often asked which people lived on the slopes and had those beautiful gardens. But the Batooro royals could say in Kiswahili language that "*wale ni wa gonjwa*" meaning those are sick. When the missionaries wanted to build schools and Hospitals to serve the people on the slopes of the mountain, the batoro royals replied, "Those are monkeys" [Alnaes, 1996; 294].

When Cyril Makoma grew up, he went to a catholic school and trained as a teacher and later became the headmaster of Nsenyi

Junior School from 1940 –1955. In 1956, while he was headmaster of Katwe primary school, he complained to the Toro Kingdom for the execution of his father, Tibamwenda. As a response to his grievances, "the Toro Kingdom appointed him sub-county chief of Karambi" [Yona Balyaghe, Oct. 2000; 38]. The Batoro leadership sensed danger when in the person of Cyril; they could have old wounds opened. They then quickly promoted him to serve in the magistrate Court office. This ended the aspiration of the Baswagha to inherit the Bakonzo/Bamba throne. Those who were on the forefront of the negotiations and pressure were frustrated and gave up the whole scheme. Almost thirty years later, a new generation of think tanks surfaced and revived the struggle for freedom and human rights. From 1954, Isaya Mukirane was involved in the Bakonzo Life History research, and as a Muhira clan leader and a trained teacher, he was agreed upon as the leader of a revolution, which would revive the grievances, aired by the Bakonzo traditional leaders; three of whom had been hanged thirty years earlier. The Baswagha and Basu clan leaders blessed the crowning of Isaya, a muhira by clan, because among those who should have been crown as clan leaders were Cyril Makoma, a Musu by clan, and Basikania, son of Mukeri. These two refused to be crowned together with Isaya because they feared to die like Nyamutswa, Kapoli and Tibamwenda. It is from this brave Isaya, that we get the child Charles Kisembo Mumbere who later became 'king' with a revolutionary vision.

In 1969 the former regent Mr. Mwambala died and a certain Bawalana came on the scene. He planned to stage a palace coup by trying to sideline Charles, take over the home of Isaya, had a child with Isaya's wife and introduced a kind of religious cult, which was not common to what Charles had grown to know. This scheme by Bawalana caused a lull in the fighting, there was some relative peace until Charles stood his ground in 1970 and threw Bawalana out of the palace. He later received rigorous military training by Amin's deserters who fled the army in 1976 after the Entebbe raid by the Israel commandoes who had come to rescue their hostages.

Insiders and not commoners only knew the myth surrounding the kingdom. To date the mythology still reigns around the kingdom, the myth has lived among the people, and this same myth has made them united around the kingdom for years. After King Charles drove Bawalana away from the palace, he devised a method of ruling which became a mystery to everyone. He became both a king and a military leader. It was very difficult to find him in one place as well he tended to live in several palaces. There was no specific headquarters, although the name Buhikira Royal palace has often been floated. Even in Harissburg USA we had a :buhikira rayal palace. It was extremely hard for any common person to know how the "kingdom" operated. They had a mechanism of collecting taxes but the accountability of those taxes was never known to many.

There was enormous fear of the movement. Whenever soldiers of the king were sighted in any neigbourhood, people often fled because either they feared to pay the tax or to be asked to carry food for the establishment. Insiders only knew the myth surrounding the kingdom. To date the myth still reigns around the kingdom, the myth has lived among the people, and this same myth has made them united around the kingdom for years.

The bakonzo have seen this kingdom as a tool to highlight their grievances notably neglect and abuse of human rights by the then toro kingdom to the central Ugandan government. Political leaders have manipulated the people and used this myth of the revolution to gain votes from the public, because what comes from the mouth of the throne is generally respected by the people of the districts of Bundibugyo and Kasese. Indeed the mythology around this kingdom has brought dignity to a people who were least known in the country.

Mighty leaders like Amin and Obote who had trained armies were not able to penetrate their intelligence into the obusinga kingdom. A few selected individual around the King himself only knew the mechanism through which the kingdom was run. Researchers have written papers about this movement, but nobody has been able to come face to face with where the establishment was being governed. During the negotiations to bring the rebellion to a stop, the Uganda people's congress government used Amon Bazira, MP and Amos Kambere MP to broker a peace deal. Amon Bazira used to come with huge amounts of money to give to the kingdom so that they stop collecting taxes from civilian population. We were however never allowed to come close to where the central governance was located. Irema Ngoma's father used to hide in what was called the furthest private cave. But for Charles, nobody knows if he even had a private cave.

CHAPTER 8

"Idi Amin (also known as Idi Amin Dada) was the nutty, ruthless dictator of the African nation of Uganda during the 1970s. He started out as a soldier in the British colonial army in 1946 and became one of its first Ugandan commissioned officers. Amin rose through the ranks and was eventually made the army's chief of staff under Uganda's first president, Milton Obote. In 1971 Amin overthrew Obote and seized power."

It is 2:00 A.M pacific time, August 16th 2003 on the Pacific Coast of North America. I am wide awake watching late night television. The Canadian broadcasting Corporation [CBC] announces the death of a renowned world dictator. The news hit headlines. "Idi Amin dada was dead after one month in coma in a Saud Arabian Hospital." The Canadian Broadcasting Corporation newscaster read; "He called himself His Excellency Dr. Idi Amin Dada, V.C. DSO, M.C, King of Scotland, Life President of Uganda and Conqueror of The British Empire."[cbctv 2003] What the Western media did not know was that Amin was Al-Hajji, he was also Chancellor of Makerere University and in 1975 he was the chairman of Organization of African Unity. All those titles used to come after his name especially when the local news were being read in on Uganda radio and television,

Amin was a world dictator, no doubt about that and sometimes referred to as the buffoon of Africa and a cannibal; he was responsible for the death of thousands of people in Uganda including the Arch Bishop of Uganda's Anglican church; he is believed to have murdered his own wife, one of several; but to some Ugandans he was a savior and a Pan Africanist. Once you follow his speeches and ideology, you will learn that Amin lacked coherence in his policies but they were all geared at a better Uganda in a united African. He just did not know how to articulate his ideas. He was not educated enough to even reason politically let alone intellectually. **He just did not know how to rule.** As he took power, he inherited written programs left behind by Milton Obote and since he was semi illiterate, he had quite a hard time filling up the puzzle and fitting in Obote's wide shoes. He missed his point however when he turned against his enemies with an iron feast and his agents brutally killed and maimed many. Amin took power in Uganda on January 25, 1971. At that time the bakonzo and Bamba had almost exhausted all avenues with the government of Milton Obote to secure peace and respect for human rights in their area. They had resorted to wanton fighting even among themselves notwithstanding their target, to secure for themselves a United Kingdom separate from that of the Batooro. Since Kingdoms had ceased to exist by 1967, the Bakonzo/Bamba had shifted course and were now demanding for a separate district. To them the whole idea was to move away from the administration of the Batooro. As soon as Idi Amin ceased power by the barrel of the gun, he declared a cease fire with the Rwenzuru, because he had been the army commander and knew the trouble he would face as president if he did not declare cease fire with King Charles Kisembo Iremangoma.

Irema Ngoma, King of the Banyarwenzururu however, ignored Amin's offer of the cease fire and went on burning Bakonzo huts and rolling stones when ever Amin's forces came to the mountain areas. The boarder area between Kasese and Kabarole and between Bwamba and Kabarole on the other side of the mountain became hostile areas and almost a no go zone. The youthful King Irema Ngoma was often seen on the frontline with his soldiers fighting anyone who opposed the kingdom and anyone who refused to pay the Rwenzururu tax. The Rwenzururu fighters were planning to take the fighting all the way to Muzizi River in Kabarole district, a river they believed was the boarder of the Kingdom before Kasagama took it over and handed it over to the Batoro.

The population in both Kasese and Bundibughyo were generally thrilled to see Obote go and Amin take over. As there were jubilations in the whole country celebrating the departure of Milton Obote, there were skepticism among the Rwenzuru leadership about the arrival of Amin, a man who in 1968 and 69 had presided over the burning and destruction of property belonging to Banyarwenzururu in the rwenzori region. The council of elders who surrounded the Irema Ngoma as advisers did not trust him even though he was now President of the Republic of Uganda. Amin had been both field commander and at the same time the Army Chief of Staff. So most of the decisions Obote took were based on the advices Amin gave him. He partly was to blame for failure to bring peace in the region. While members of the Democratic Party in Parliament were calling for the Bakonzo to be wiped out so that the area could be declared into a National park, Amin was in full gear commanding his National troops to kill, rape and maim innocent civilians. They did these horrible acts of gross human rights violation because the Bakonzo either failed or refused to show them the way that lead to the Irema Ngoma's palace. Some members of the Democratic Party in Parliament even stooped so low as to call for the castration of the Bakonzo tribe so that they stop producing more children. In spite of all these, the Bakonzo and Bamba did not resent the Democratic Party, as I discussed in previous chapters.

Amin, during his takeover speech declared, "I am not a politician, I am a professional solider". [Uganda Argus Jan/26, 1971] But when you look at the way he handled the Banyarwenzururu matters, it was typical political tactics. In 1972 while people were still celebrating his raise to power, some young Bakonzo boys and men decided that in order for them to be noticed and present their demands in person, they will 'walk' to state house Entebbe to officially thank him for removing Obote who had refused to separate them from the Batooro. They would then demand that he does the noblest of thing; grant them separation. Volunteers were recruited and quite a sizable number of people made the trek to the State House Entebbe, a journey of almost 300 kilometers. They walked through Fort Portal, Mubende, Mityana, Kampala and then Entebbe. Amin received them and letter gave them a plane back to Kasese. As a professional soldier, he met with this delegation dressed in military fatigue and told the youth that he would be meeting with the elders of both Kasese and Bwamba.

A delegation chaired by Mr. Daudi Muhindo a.k.a Isebira prepared to meet with Amin to present a memorandum representing all the Banyarwenzururu. Among the delegation were Mr. Ezironi Bitaaba and Hajji Muhamoud Baluku. The Irema Ngoma Privy Council did not approve this delegation and did not contribute any suggestions to ideas and points that were put in the memorandum. Nevertheless, Daudi Muhindo and his team went a head and prepared to meet with Amin and push for a separate district for the Banyarwenzururu.

When Idi Amin took power, most Ugandans were worried about what Obote had pronounced at Lugogo in 1969, at the Uganda Peoples Congress annual delegates conference. He had announced the "Common Man's Charter". The majority of Ugandans did not understand what would come out of this so-called Common Man's Charter, a policy statement that would have steered the country towards socialist progressive programs.

Amin used this as one of the reasons why he took over government. But the more painful question has remained: was this Amin's idea to take power? Throughout his leadership in the late 1960s, Dr. Apolo Milton Obote was consolidating his grip on power and introducing democratic legislation that was to shake the colonial interests. Although he was not a Castrol or a Kaddafi, his common man's charter I mentioned earlier and the nationalization of almost 80 British companies were not welcome in by Her Majesty's government. Obote was on the point of changing not only the constitution but the whole political system when the coup occurred. Uganda was a vital source of raw materials, and for this reason was not about to be permitted to determine its own political development at the expense of the entrenched colonial interest. Therefore plans were put in place by Britain, Israel, and America to remedy the growing situation. As they planned to remove Dr. Obote from power, they had to quickly find a possible successor who would serve their best interest. Idi Amin became that choice. The British knew him since he served as a non commissioned officer in the British colonial regiment as well as with the British as they were suppressing the rebellion in Mau Mau area of Kenya. Amin as he was aided to take power, he appointed a cabinet of intellectuals who were opposed to the Uganda Peoples Congress Party. He brought in people like Edward Rugumayo, Abu Mayanja, Luimbazi Zake, Wanume Kibedi, Charles Ondonga, Henry Kyemba and others but none from the ranks of the Bakonzo and Bamba. This was partly because he could not find an "intellectual" who was ministerial material. The Bakonzo had just had their sixth graduate from Makerere University since independence.

Uganda, at the time Amin took over, had four administrative regions, thus Northern, Western, Eastern and Buganda regions. There were 18 districts in total. When the Bakonzo elders presented their memorandum, it had so many demands, but the most notable ones were the demand for a separate district, the establishment of secondary schools and a district hospital. Since independence there were no secondary schools in Kasese and Bundibugyo and there was no hospital in Kasese. This perhaps explains why at his take over, there were barely six men who had graduated from University in the whole district.

Although Amin, at his inauguration as President, had proclaimed that he was a professional solider and not a politician, the Bakonzo case put him to test and was forced to make a political decision that affected the entire country. He made a determination that if he answered the demands of the Bakonzo he would have the Batooro jumping up in arms and resisting the solved equation. Indeed he would become unpopular among the Batooro because he would have pleased their traditional enemies. As well, he would be setting up a bad precedent by opening up a window where by any disagreement among any tribe in Uganda a call for separation would ensue, which means he would have a handful of grievances coming from the diverse tribes of the entire country.

So he took off the military hat and put on the "political" one and made a political decision. He decided that in order to solve the burning problems of the Bakonzo and Bamba he was not to give them the schools or hospitals, but was to allow them to be governed as separate districts. Instead of announcing that the Bakonzo and Bamba were given separate districts from Toro, Amin announced that every District in Uganda would be divided into two for easy administration and that Toro would be divided into three. He started with Ankole which now gave birth to East Ankole and West Ankole. He divided Acholi District to now become North Acholi and south Acholi districts, and for Toro, he divided it to become Rwenzori District, Kabarole and Semuliki districts. One will notice that Most of the Districts in Uganda kept their originals names save for the additions of either East or West or North and South. For the Bakonzo, the name Toro had to be eliminated from their vocabulary and that brought sense of satisfaction and comfort among the Bakonzo and Bamba who now praised Amin as "the Man" finally at last. Towards the end of 1973 the District of Rwenzori was born and Maja Alur became the first district commissioner.

A professional solider, now turned Politician tried to solve the question of the Banyarwenzuru, but this did not please the "Irema Ngoma privy council" which denounced the announcement as a mire fuss. They argued that Amin did not actually give them their district. First they argued that the boarders were not defined and that much of their land remained with Toro. They also argued that the district was empty without indigenous people working in it. "It was like giving you a match box without matches", said one of the privy councilors. At this point the war would rage on and Irema Ngoma would continue to fight until his people realized and assumed full leadership of their district, so to say. In 1973, even when the district had been granted, some Bakonzo scholars from Makerere University decided that they would try to convince the leadership of the Rwenzuru Kingdom to abandon fighting, which had caused untold suffering among their people. One among these scholars was Mr. Kireru who made several efforts to try to meet with the Irema Ngoma's privy council to see if he could discuss the idea of abandoning hostilities and concentrating efforts to fighting by the book and by the pen. Kireru as one of the leaders of Rwenzori Students Association, made several attempts to climb the mountains in an effort to seek audience with the King himself. He was being sent by the Daudi Muhindo's committee to arrange a meeting with the Privy Council. At this point it is believed that the Privy Council was expecting to meet Daudi Muhindo and was prepared to arrest him for going a head to meet with Amin without consulting them.

Mr. Kereru

Instead they saw the young Kireru coming uphill. On that fateful occasion while he was climbing the mountains in Kyanzuki, Kilembe sub county, he was arrested and later that day killed by the very people he thought would lead him to the King. He was mourned greatly by the local people, the school children and the students at the university. This happened in 1973 after Amin had announced the subdivisions of districts and Bakonzo and Bamba had benefited from this announcement of the new districts. Irema Ngoma continued to resist the rule of Idi Amin because his privy council contended that the central government had given us the district without resources and the Bakonzo would not even get jobs. The core issue here was not the district, but was lack of education and education institutions, hospitals, and the infrastructure. The king himself was un educated. These services had to be in place for anyone to assume that development had come to an area. When confronted with the question of killing people even the educated few, Irema Ngoma has always defended his soldiers' actions that they did not intend to harm indigenous people, but that during any struggle, there is always loss of life and he has since apologized for such un intentional losses of human life and property. Mr. Kireru's death scared off scholars from making further attempts to persuade the Irema Ngoma to abandon fight and causing untold suffering to the people he claimed to be his subjects. But with the myth surrounding the Kingdom growing, so support for the Rwenzururu movement continued to grow.

CHAPTER 9

The Gate way to Education –
The third class train voyage

As the Rwenzururu rebellion was raging on, the parents in Kasese and Bundibugyo did not relent on education. They did not care whether Fort Portal did not admit their children in the government and private school that were already established there. There was one gate through which some daring parents and their children capitalized on. This was the Railway that joined Kampala city to Kasese. The train at that time was the only gate way to the capital city, Kampala where several day schools and private school became the main resource for the Bakonzo and Bamba to educate their children. A few of such school were Old Kampala Senior Secondary School, His Highness the Aga Khan secondary school, Kololo senior secondary school, Mengo Secondary school, Kitante High school and Kibuli Moslem High school. The private schools included Bashir High school and Muhmoud High school. The graduates of these school formed the elite class in Rwenzori and Bwamba. The students who went to these schools passed through untold hardships in order to acquire an education. Between 1970 and 1974 the education system left behind by the UPC regime was still functional and the bursary structure was still working. Because Bursaries were sent to schools from each district, it was mandatory that some money were sent to government schools whether they were day schools or boarding schools. The amount was allotted according to students per district. Therefore the kids who were in the Kampala schools mostly came from Kasese and not Toro. This means when it came to giving out bursaries to students who came from Toro and attended say Old Kampala Secondary School, the majority happened to be coming from the Bakonzo land. This is the only way we benefited from the bursary scheme. Each student was allocated two hundred Uganda shillings and fees was in most cases was one hundred and forty shillings for day schools. Each student would then be invited to the headmasters office to be told that they received a bursary of 200/- which covered the school fees. The student had a choice to withdraw the 60/- or save it for next semester if they were unsure whether they would receive more assistance. In most cases the students chose to withdraw the balance. This in most of the cases was the only pocket money they would survive on for the entire three months of school. Some of these students just left their home in Bukonzo with a bag of about 40 kilograms of cassava flour [kaunga], about 10 kilograms of beans and about 5 kilograms of dry ground nuts that would last them three months. They would arrive in Kampala where they knew nobody, find a rented accommodation or some home stay of some sort. For those who attended Kyambogo college school, they used to stay in boys quarters of teachers houses. The same applied to those who attended Mengo secondary school. Those who went to Old Kampala and Aga Khan School did not have this privilege because these were purely Indians schools. It was difficult to find accommodation from teachers' quarters, therefore African students, who were mainly from Kasese ganged together and lived in a suburb called Nakulabye while other lived in Kasubu. These were central places which served Old Kampala, Mengo and Aga Khan. Transportation to Kampala was cheap. Students paid concession tickets at 2.75/- in the third class. The full fare in third class was 5.25/-. The parents who accompanied their first time students to Kampala could not afford to travel in second or first class. So they sat with their children in the third class. The journey took exactly 12 hours and it was always over night. Students left Kasese at 6:00pm and arrived in Kampala either at 6:00am or there about. During this time, the train system was efficient and enabled parents to educate their children. One such student who benefited from this train system is the second Bishop of Rwenzori diocese the Rt. Rev. Jackson Nzerebende, a graduate of H.H.The Aga Khan School [later known as Kampala High School]. Mr. Jackson went to Bukuku theological college after high school and was ordained a priest and served in the newly created diocese of south rwenzori. He later joined the University of Mokono to graduate with a degree in Theology and later was elected the second Bishop of South Rwenzori diocese, the creation of which I will discuss in a later chapter. There are other persons who benefited from the gateway. The first indigenous person to occupy the office of District Treasurer, Mr. Leo Bwambale was a graduate of Muhmoud high school, a private school that admitted students from Kasese who did not find places in the Kampala school. One of the young people, who walked from Kasese to Entebbe to see Idi Amin, had just dropped out of Bashir High school near Wandengeya in Kampala. His name was Matayo. After having a meeting with Idi Amin, he was appointed to work in the Queen Elizabeth Park as a game ranger. Some of the girls who did not have money to travel to Kampala and probably did not pass very well to be officially admitted just jumped on the train to go and loiter in Kampala until they found a school that would take them. It did not matter whether they got a private school or any day government school; what mattered here was that they needed post primary education. The schools were not available in their district; they had to look for them in a capital city which did not discriminate. In 1972 when Amin expelled the Asians, the three schools which were predominantly Indians schools, i.e. Kololo High school, Aga Khan secondary school, and Old Kampala secondary school became depopulated. The most affected one was the Aga Khan. The ministry of education had to move some streams from Old Kampala and Kololo to come and fill up classes at the Aga Khan, because they needed to keep all the schools running. A few boys from Kasese who attended Old Kampala were moved to Aga Khan. During the following year, 1973, admissions were more flexible so that more Africans were admitted into these Kampala schools. This encouraged more of the Kasese boys and girls to just travel to Kampala to find schools. For some who did not get enough fees to find a school in Kampala, or simply dropped out after a year or two in senior, they joined the Amin army as soldiers. Others joined the police after senior four if they could not go to higher school certificate. Because there was that bond of students from Kasese, those who joined the army would frequently visit their friends who were still going to school. Most of the students who came from Kasese did not bring enough food rations to last them the entire three months. Therefore their friends who had joined the army came to their rescue by bringing them some of the army ration. There were so many ways these boys survived in the capital city, but all in all they acquired some level of education. The Rwenzori boys and girls will never forget the train that transported them to Kampala and the support they received from each other as they lived far away from home to secure an education. As we received the district, graduates from these Kampala schools actually came to work in Kasese. Mr. Leo Bwambale, a graduate of Mahmud secondary school became the first mukonzo district treasure and with him came many boys to work as clerks and administrative assistants. Maja Alur was the first district commissioner appointed by Idi Amin to head the district. He was a native of West Nile district. He encouraged as many qualified indigenous boys to apply for jobs at the district level.

CHAPTER 10

**From the National Teachers university to
National Assembly of Uganda
1978 -1984**

March 1978 I graduated as high school teacher and was posted to
teach in Kigezi High School situated in the district of Kabale. I taught
senior two and three. While at Kigezi high school, I did some statistics
of students leaving this particular school to be admitted to Makerere
University. In that year, 1978 we had 68 boys and girls who sat for their
Higher school certificate Exam. Demographically, out of 68 students,
60 were natives of Kigezi district; therefore they were Bakiga by tribe.
We had one from Lango, one from Kasese, one from Kabarole, two
from Buganda, and three from Mbarara district. Out of 68 students, we
had 60 students who passed very well and were eligible to be admitted
to the university. Out of the 60, 52 were Bakiga coming from Kigezi
district. This told me that because the school was locally situated in
Kigezi, the majority of the students who go to that school are from the
local areas and therefore the majority to be admitted to the university
will come from that local district. When I looked at other schools
around the same district, they had similar statistics. So in one year,
because we had three secondary schools in one district all offering high

school certificate, there was at least an average of 50 students coming from each school going to the university. This now meant that in one year we had at least 150 students coming from one district plus those students who opted to go to other schools in Uganda. When you look at the total number of students from Kabale, the Bakiga being admitted to Makerere University, the number jumped to at least 200 because 50 catered for students who were in schools like Ntare, Budo, Gayaza, Namiliango, Nyakasura who otherwise came from Kigezi district as their home.. Now because Kasese did not have a secondary school at the time, we were only able to send at least 5 students to Makerere compared to 200 from a similar nearby district. So where is the equality and justice here? Who do we blame for this imbalance? The answer is in lack of schools. I discussed this situation with my mentor Mr. Enoch Muhindo who was at the time lecturing at the Kyambogo University College where I had just graduated. He agreed with me as I shared the statistics with him because he had been a teacher at Kigezi high school before he went to Kyambogo. We both agreed that the answer lied within us. We had to open schools ourselves and stop blaming the Toro Kingdom, because it was long gone, and we would be shading crocodile tears if we continued to place the blame on the Batoro.

In 1979 the war to overthrow the dictator Mr. Dada Amin was raging on and we prayed hard for its success. When the city of Mbarara fell to the fighting forces that were composed of Tanzanian soldiers and the Ugandan exiles, there were celebrations in Kabale as we saw Amin's soldiers fleeing for their lives. Brig. David Oyite Ojok was in charge of the Masaka axis heading for the capital Kampala while Yoweri Museveni and Rurangaranga were in charge of the western axis responsible to see that there was no mayhem in the west as Amin's soldiers were fleeing. On April 11, 1979 we heard the announcement on radio Uganda, the voice was that of David Oyite Ojok announcing that Kampala city had fallen and that Amin had fled. A UNLF – Uganda National Liberation Front was formed and Yosufu Lule was declared president as elected by exiles during the Moshi conference. Yoweri Museveni was defense minister in that government, David Oyite Ojok was chief of staff and Major Edward Rurangaranga was deputy minister of Local government. As the UNLF government's army the

UNLA was sweeping all cities of the remnants of Amin's notorious boys, party leaders were sending their carders to begin introducing their party policies to schools and communities in preparation for the promised elections. At Kigezi high school we were visited by two middle aged individuals who introduced themselves as Ruhakana-Rugunda and Amama-Mbabazi respectively. They requested to speak to students in the main hall, and we allowed them. Later they spoke to the staff and we fired them with questions. These two individuals were at one time UPC youth wingers before Amin over threw their government in 1971. Now they were coming as members of a new party they called UPM – Uganda patriotic Movement. Within a couple of months, 68 days to be precise the UNLF government had fallen and Prof. Yosufu Lule had been deposed and replaced by former UPC attorney general Mr. Godfrey Lukongwa Binaisa QC.

After Rugunda and Amama Mbabazi had left our school, we realized that the entire student body did not buy into their philosophy. We opened up a UPC branch at the school and we elected an executive committee of which I was elected secretary for this branch. The UPM did not have enough members to open a branch at the school. A month after we established the UPC branch I was visited by two individuals from Kasese district with a letter from Amon Bazira.

Amon Bazira was the Director General of Intelligence in Lule's government and later in Binaisa's government. President Yusufu Lule appointed him on recommendation of the National consultative Council of which Edward Rugumayo was the chairman. Amon Bazira was a native of Bwera Sub County and was the first graduate to come from Bwera in 1970. During Amin's time, he was doing private business as an advertising consultant on Kampala road opposite the general post office. He was also doing under ground intelligence work for the UPC and sending private massages to Tanzania. He successfully did this without being detected by Amin's killer squad using his advertising business as the cover. In 1978 around about February, Amin's intelligence zeroed up on him and he was finally netted and locked up in Naguru military unit under the notorious Ali Towili. He was going to be killed but was saved by the king of Rwanda, King Kigeri, a friend of Amin Dada. The King petitioned Amin by pleading for Bazira's release. Kigeri told Amin that the enemies of the Bakonzo were framing Bazira. Kigeri gave the example of how Bazarabusa was killed in fake motor accident, a plot believed to have been organized by the enemies of the Bakonzo/ Basongoro. Amin listen and believed the King and Amon Bazira was released. As he left Naguru police torture chambers, he run to Kasese and lived in hiding in Bwera among his Basongora tribe until Amin was overthrown. During all this time, he was rarely seen in his native land, probably as a cover so that he is not pointed out to the bad guys. He quickly moved into Kampala as Oyite Ojok announced the fall of the regime.

In 1979 the Rwenzuru fighters under 'king' Charles Irema Ngoma seized the city of Kasese and chased away all the non-bakonzo civil and public servants. They staged their front line on river Rwimi and killed many batoro who were attempting to cross over to Kasese. The Rwenzururu soldiers acquired many arms from the fleeing soldiers. Kasese district was the gateway and escape route for the Amin soldiers who ended up in the Congo, [Zaire at that time]. One of the conditions to allow them safe escape was the surrender of their arms to the Rwenzururu soldiers. On the central government side, we had the TPDF – Tanzanian Peoples' Defense

Forces taking care of the peace in the area. As soon as they realized that the Bakonzo were fighting amongst themselves, they ignored them because for them all they were after were the fleeing Amin's soldiers. The TPDF was not ready to medel into internal political issue. This helped Charles Kisembo Iremangom organize his troops and seize control over many areas of the district. Local people as well as the Rwenzururu army had disarmed most of the fleeing soldiers. Rwenzururu was transformed from a rag tag arm of spears and clubs to a rebel army with sub machine guns and motors.

Mr. Edward Rugumayo was the chairman of the NCC. Kasese had a representative in the NCC. His name was Dr. Henry Bwambale. Mr. Rugumayo summoned a meeting comprised of the Member of the NCC, Dr. Bwambale, the Army chief of Staff Maj. General David Oyite Ojok plus the Director General of intelligence Mr. Amon Bazira. They met to see how they could resolve the conflict that was brewing up on by the boarder of Kasese and Kabarole districts, plus they wanted to recapture Kasese back from the Irema Ngoma rebels. Rugumayo is a native of Kabarole while Bazira and Bwambale were natives of Kasese. Oyite Ojok was the neutral figure in this meeting at the same time he commanded the army that would be responsible for quelling the rebellion. There was civil unrest in Kasese and Kabarole, the administration had broken down, and the government had a duty to restore peace. After this meeting, Rugumayo ordered David Oyite Ojok and Amon Bazira plus the member of NCC Mr. Bwambale to visit the district and see if they could talk to the Rwenzuru leadership to stop the insurgencies. A military solution was not the answer since this had been tried before and had miserably failed.

The country was preparing for an election the following year 1980. These people were charged with a responsibility of stabilizing the region so that a peaceful election could be conducted. You will note here that David Oyite Ojok was a member of Uganda Peoples' Congress, and so was Amon Bazira. Dr. Henry was a member of the Democratic Party. So we had two people here both coming from Bwera each with different political agenda; to try to stop the Rwenzuru from fighting the Batoro. Amon Bazira had made several contacts with Irema Ngoma during the time he was hiding from Amin after he left Naguru. So at least he had a starting point. He meet the Rwenzuru leaders together with Oyite Ojok. Since they were both in business of taking care of national security, they chose to meet the Rwenzururu leaders at their front line. They excluded Dr. Henry Bwambale because he was a civilian. They used their military muscle to convince and lure the Rwenzururu fighters into a meeting at Hima cement factory. At this meeting they agreed with the fighters to declare and honor a cease-fire. Under the conditions of a cease-fire, Amon Bazira promised to negotiate with the government to allow Rwenzururu leaders to appoint chiefs in Kasese District, as well as getting an indigenous Mukonzo to be head of the district as District commissioner. If this deal went through, he was to be the first District Commissioner to come from Kasese district since independence. He had to be a person acceptable to the Irema Ngoma Privy Council as well as having the qualification acceptable to the public service commission. Amon Bazira quickly suggested the name of Mr. Blasio Maate, Headmaster of Bwera primary school and was acceptable to the Rwenzururu negotiators. However, he was not acceptable to the public service commission, because he was not qualified. He was a grade three teacher only acceptable by the teaching service commission, and not the public service commission. He nevertheless had reputable personality among the Bakonzo, he had been jailed during the Omukama of toro upraising and had been exiled into a jail in Northern Uganda, because he was with Isaya Mukirane in the initial revolt. This was the only name that would resonate well among the Bakonzo tribes' men as well as the Rwenzururu leadership.

So Mr. Amon Bazira had to use his political skill to convince the ministry of public service to waive the conditions and allow Mr. Maate to be appointed District Commissioner if this was a recipe to quell a rebellion. It was an uphill task, but worth the gamble because this was better than the shedding of blood that was still raging on between the Batooro and the Bakonzo. Bazira undertook this gamble by himself leaving Dr. Bwambale Henry out of the picture. This would be a heavy political potato for Amon Bazira as he knew at the back of his mind that a district commissioner would be very important during the political nominations.

In 1979 Mr. Bulasio Maate became the first Mukonzo to occupy the office of District Commissioner. He replaced Edward Sempebwa who had been appointed by the public service commission during the late days of Idi Amin.

The Irema Ngoma council was allowed to appoint two Saza or County chiefs and Mr. Kamabu Yonasani occupied the office at Kisinga county headquarters while Mr. Paul Rwibende occupied the office at Rukoki county headquarters. Both these men were unqualified for these offices, but this was necessary in order to stop the blood shed that was raging on along the Rwimi River.

Calm returned to Kasese under Blasio Maate. The Rwenzururu leadership observed the cease fire. Amon Bazira had convinced them to stop collecting taxes from the population. He had opted to bringing them hard cash from the government to sustain the leadership with a core of a few soldiers who stayed with the King. Majority of the soldiers were appointed as local askaris at the county and sub county headquarters as those of the central government had fled during the time Rwenzururu was in control of the townships. Bazira used his special branch and intelligence account to draw heavy sums of money to give to the Rwenzururu leaders. This helped Bazira build his confidence and trust among the local leaders as well as the Privy Council. There was no single person other than Bazira who had the leverage to marshal huge amounts of shillings to give to the Rwenzuru leadership. They had stopped collecting money from civilians. It would take a heavy weight with government connections to get the huge amounts for money and to be able to account for it in a security language. The president's office was fully supportive of every move we took. Minsiter Chris Rwakasisi and Amon Bazira were both in the business of National security and therefore they new how to maneouver and get away with huge sums with minimum if not private accountability.

The following year was a year of campaigns. Mr. Amon Bazira resigned his job as director general of intelligence because he saw an opportunity to serve his district and would use the Rwenzururu leaders to run his campaign since he had established a good relationship with them and convinced them that Uganda Peoples Congress had the capacity to win the elections. Dr. Obote had just returned from exile on May 27 1980 and was given a reception that befitted a head of state; a strong message to the electorate that he would win the forth coming elections. At this time Godfrey Lukongwa Binaisa had been removed from power as president after 9 months and been replaced with a more hardliner UPC die-hard, Mr. Paul Muwanga. Yoweri Museveni had been reduced to less important ministry of Regional corporation and vice chairman to Paul Muwanga. It is from this point of view that Bazira started looking for individuals who would work with him to see Uganda Peoples Congress win seats in Kasese. He sent a letter to me in Kabale inviting me to meet with him in Kasese to discuss the possibility of standing for the UPC party.

I was in the middle of giving exams at the end of 1979 and I was due to travel to Kampala to mark the O'level exams. I instead traveled to Kasese, met with Amon Bazira who briefed me about the strategy of using the Rwenzururu leaders to run the UPC campaign. I quickly saw the opportunity to introduce my Education agenda to the government. I accepted his request, returned to Kabale to wind up the school year, resigned my teaching position and joined Bazira in the bid to see UPC win seats in Kasese, so that we can talk about education, unemployment, indigenous people getting jobs, and peace in our district. Literacy, job creation and peace was to be my campaign theme.

Bazira had held a few meetings with the Rwenzururu leadership and had suggested to the 'king' Irema Ngoma that for them to have a voice in the government, the entire movement had to support the Uganda Peoples' Congress. Bazira had explained to the leadership why he thought UPC would win the election. He had explained that Obote had returned from Tanzania, from where the Ugandan rebels came with TPDF to remove Idi Amin. He had explained that David Oyite Ojok who was the chief of staff was from Obote's tribe and played a major role in Removing Amin and bringing Obote home. He also mentioned that Paul Muwanga who was now the chairman of the military commission was a staunch UPC supporter and several cabinet ministers at the time were mostly from Uganda Peoples congress party. It was therefore common knowledge that if UPC won the elections, a district had to have UPC members of parliament in order to have a voice in this government. This was the only way the Rwenzururu grievances would be heard if they returned UPC members to parliament. The Irema Ngoma Privy council agreed and were ready to listen to directions from Amon Bazira as to how they would help promote the UPC party in a predominantly DP area. During prior elections in 1961 and 1962 Toro district had voted for the Democratic Party and had remain so even during the 1980 elections. Kasese and Bundibugyo were part of Toro and even though they had separated by way of districts, they still carried the sentiments of the Democratic Party. Bazira had to break this trend in order to be returned as UPC. One of the suggestions he gave to the King was for the Privy Council to announce that the people will support only one party. Having members of the Privy Council attend public rallies that were organized by the Uganda Peoples congress party would reinforce this declaration. They could have chosen to say no, but they believed in what Bazira told them. In actual sense, the UPC first had to convince the Rwenzururu movement leaders before they went after the general population. Bazira already knew his own people's history by the way they voted in the past. So all he wanted was to have a strong bargain with the movement while isolating the democratic party of Dr. Henry Bwambale. The Rwenzururu movement relented because then they knew that through Bazira they would have direct access to the top leadership should the UPC win the elections. They had seen this evidently when he facilitated them to meet with the chief of staff and later with President Godfrey Binaisa. This was the first time Rwenzururu leaders had ever had direct talks with the President of Uganda. Bazira had something to offer unlike Dr. Bwambale, a member of the Democratic Party who sat in the National Cconsultative Council; the defacto parliament at the time when the war was raging on at the Kasese and Toro boarder. Bazira had used his military intelligence cap to build confidence among the Rwenzururu, unlike Bwambale, a civilian with more of an academic background. He depended on the historic voting of the people and assumed that the Democratic Party would ride high as it had always done in the past. He was wrong as he was already out maneuvered by the shrewd Bazira.

CHAPTER 11

The 1980 election

Dr. Apollo Milton Obote returned from exile in Tanzania on May 27th 1980. He landed in Mbarara airport and transported in a huge motorcade to Bushenyi as he was accorded presidential reception. I traveled from Kabale to attend this mammoth rally. From here I went to Kasese and met with Amon Bazira. We moved to Kyarumba, my hometown centre with him to assess the support UPC had among the people. As soon as we arrived at the trading centre, a small crowd of people assembled; among them were Mr. Christopher Tembo and Banginalia John. Both of these gentle men had been with Irema Ngoma in the mountains as a teacher and member of Privy Council respectively.

Bazira and I addressed them briefly and informed them that there was need for them to organize a sub county UPC committee, which would be responsible to nominate me when time comes. We moved on to Kisinga and we found similar small crowds. The party was indeed weak among the population. All they knew was the symbol of the hoe, which represented the DP. We realized that ours would be an uphill task to introduce the people to the symbol of the 'open hand' which was the UPC. At the same time we were mindful of the new party, which had been launched in Kampala by the Minister of regional corporation Mr. Yoweri Museveni, and the party was called Uganda Patriotic Movement [UPM]. Majority of the leadership were the youths. This new party attracted the former UPC youth wingers who were looking for new ideas, and wanted to change from the old UPC. They recruited all those who did not have any party affiliations.

The traditional parties that are UPC and DP were formed on religious grounds, therefore all the moderates who felt that they could not go to DP just because they were Catholics or go to UPC just because they were Protestants ended up joining the UPM. This is where we find the Hon. Crispus Kiyonga. The 1980 elections in Kasese was yet to take an interesting turn as the Rwenzururu movement took control of the campaigns. After our meeting with residents of Kyarumba I was summoned to the king's palace. A Mr. Yohana Ngike came specifically to lead me to the palace. I was to meet with the Irema ngoma first to introduce my self and secondly to inform the King about my capabilities as a prospective Member of Parliament who would represent the Kingdom and thirdly to explain to the King what I intended to do for the people. I climbed the mountains for the first time with Ngike. We moved through Kisinga up to Kalingwe up to Kahindangoma where I met the first road block as a sign that the King would be in the neigbourhood. I was to see the King for the first time and I did not know how he looked like. I met a young energetic man sitting on red stool surrounded by two other men whom I later found out were bodyguards. We held a mutual meeting, we understood each. I found him to be a sweet, warm middle-aged man. I told him my vision about the district and I found we shared a lot in common. We discussed the lack of educated people in our district and I explained to him that it was all because we did not have schools. He spoke some little English, but most of our conversation was held in Lukonzo. After our short discussion, we had lunch together comprised of Bundu and goat meet. I was never allowed to see the palace nor the cabinet. Whether they existed or not remained a myth as has been to many, including the present governments. When I came back, we moved to Bwera and found the former member of NCC Dr. Henry Bwambale being confronted by the Rwenzururu soldiers telling him to stop confusing people about parties. Bazira suggested that we hold a joint meeting with Dr. Bwambale to iron out our differences and look at developments that we wished to bring to Kasese through a joint initiative. Bazira suggested that we field candidate belonging to one party, which was the UPC, but Henry refused. Bazira was prepared to forward Dr. Bwambale's name to the rwenzururu leaders to represent Kasese North. But Bwambale did not accept to do politics with the rwenzururu leadership. We then aligned ourselves with the Rwenzururu leaders and encouraged them to tell the people that only one party could solve the problems of our district. We told them that in the past UPC did not handle the Rwenzururu issues just because we did not have representatives within the Party. The time was now since we had identified the problems and we had a party, which had promised to address them. We informed that king's Privy Council that they had been allowed to have a district commissioner who was a Mukonzo as well as having chiefs from within their ranks. We also informed them that there would be no government which would allow them assume the jobs they held if they did not have elected representatives within their ranks to defend them. And it was clearly obvious that any government other than UPC would dismiss them from their jobs because they were not qualified for those jobs. We then informed the masses that if this political partnership did not materialize the war would resume, and the peace that was being enjoyed would evaporate in thin air. This was a positive campaign tool for the UPC and ourselves.

The representatives of the Rwenzururu movement carried this message across the district with the UPC candidates on their sides.

When we came to Kasese Township, we found a mixture of parties, tribes and naturally with this confusion emerged. The town had more people informed about party politics than the villages where we had been. It was therefore difficult to just tell the people that we will go with one party. The Uganda Patriotic Movement was already organizing most non-Bakonzo voter to join. The Democratic Party was particularly strong here because most businessmen in the township were either from Toro or Bushenyi districts. It was common knowledge that the Batoro were traditional supporters of the Democratic Party. It was at this time that further consultations were necessary between the Rwenzururu leadership and the two of us. A meeting was held in Saad hotel in Kasese where Irema Ngoma sent his Prime Minister Mr. Yeremiya Muhongya. The district commissioner Mr. Blasio maate chaired the meeting. He was to be the returning officer and one of his tasks was to ensure that elections were conducted in a peaceful environment. At this meeting in Saad Hotel, the Rwenzururu Prime Minister delivered a message from Irema ngoma. The message was that:"Rwenzururu movement and their subject will vote for Uganda Peoples' Congress". The prime minister urged the local leaders to adhere to the 'kings' call. All chiefs were to preach the massage of UPC even though they did not know what UPC stood for. There was disagreement as to how this massage was to be carried out. However, the prime minister promised that the Rwenzururu movement would send agents or emissaries who would attend every public rally to ensure that only the UPC was introduced to the people. During this meeting, Dr. Henry Bwambale objected to this method. He subsequently walked out of the meeting and vowed to disassociate himself from the decisions of this meeting.

In August 1980, the kings emissaries stood on the boma ground of Kasese Township and announced that all non Bakonzo especially the Batoro were to leave the district with 7 days. Because chiefs from the Rwenzururu ranks manned the sub counties, this proclamation would be enforced without delay. The police was rendered useless because former Rwenzururu soldiers manned the local administration police. The three kings' emissaries went to Rukoki, Maliba, Hima and Kicwamba announcing the same massage of expelling the Batoro within 7 days. There was commotion in the district as we saw people leaving Kasese town in an exodus style. Meanwhile on the other side in Fort Portal, the Batoro leaders announced the same. All Bakonzo were to leave Fort Portal in 7 days. This mostly affected church priests. They were the only one working in Toro churches. There were no business people from Kasese who would be in Fort Portal. We saw a handful of priests leaving Toro and coming to Kasese their homeland. At that time we still had one diocese called the "the diocese of Rwenzori" where Bishop Rwakaikara was the right reverend. The RT. Rev Yonasani Kamanyire would later replace him.

At this point it was almost a scandal that the central government could not control the situation. Bazira in his effort to avoid a bloody confrontation among the Bakonzo, had hoodwinked the central government by systematically facilitating the Rwenzururu leadership take control of the entire district. The district commissioner who could order the police to intervene was handicapped because he paid more allegiance to the "king" although he represented the President of the republic of Uganda. The central government in Kampala sent two ministers to try to resolve the situation. Minister Akena P'ojok was assigned the responsibility to come and quell the situation. Hon. Akena P'ojok meet with the Rwenzururu leaders separately before he met with the political leaders. The Rwenzururu leaders plainly told him that the Batoro had to leave because they were going to overwhelmingly vote for the Democratic Party. So they were expelled to go to their homeland where they traditionally voted DP. The minister appealed to the Rwenzururu leaders to rescind their decision and stop the exodus. Mr. Akena proceeded to Kabarole to meet with the batoro leaders to tell them the same massage to stop the exodus. The situation returned to normal after two weeks of total confusion and turmoil. Those who had gone did not return, and those who were not gone yet, either went anyways or decided to stay and keep a low profile.

The Rwenzururu leaders had made their point, any non-Mokonzo who campaigned for DP or UPM would face retribution. Because

Bazira was always on public rallies where the massage of expulsion was being delivered, it was conveniently assumed that Bazira expelled the Batoro from Kasese district. This was not true because all the three candidates of the Uganda Peoples' congress were at all rallies; therefore it was wrong for the blame to be placed on one individual, Amon Bazira. The only reason why the assumption was sustained was because Bazira commanded more authority as a former Director General of National intelligence than any other person in the district plus it was through his scheme that Kasese had been controlled by the Rwenzururu authorities instead of the central government. At one of the rallies for example, Dr. Henry Bwambale was present, and as a former member of the National Consultative council, NCC, he was never associated with the Batoro exodus. During one of the meetings in which the Rwenzururu message of Batoro expulsion was spoken at Katwe, Mr. Yohana Ngike was arrested. He was put in a police cell at Katwe police station, and one policeman, a mutoro by tribe got a hammer and drove a six-foot nail into his head. He died instantly. This case was never investigated and no one was charged for this heinous crime. He was buried with this nail still in his head.

That episode of the exodus passed. The situation slowly returned to normal and campaigns resumed after the government minister had returned to Kampala.

During independence celebration on 0ctober 9th 1980 the minister of information Hon. David Anyoti represented the government. He came with a message of reconciliation. He called on the people to live together, vote together and vote for a government that would be committed to their promises. David Anyoti moved on to Fort Portal to address the same rally. We moved on with him. As soon as Bazira arrived, the crowd calling him the "lion" of Kasese booed him. We were however given the platform to greet the people. We later left before Anyoti made his speech. The situation had gradually returned to normal. After the mediation by Hon. Akena P'ojok, political parties were allowed to campaign freely in the district. We had several candidates conducting political campaigns in several townships. The two other political parties that were DP and UPM had not done their primary elections for fear of what Rwenzururu had announced. They now had very little time to organize themselves. One of the hot spots was that in Kasese town centre. This was a heavily populated area with various political opinions. The struggle was between DP and UPM because the UPC already had a candidate endorsed by the Rwenzururu movement. His name was Adam Musa Kisughu [RIP]. Kasese south was to be represented by Amos Kambere and Kasese west was to be represented by Amon Bazira. So as soon as the door was open for political campaigns, Kasese north, which had the township, had several candidates emerging as potential contenders for the Kasese north seat. Kasese north had just seen their first graduate in the person of Jorome Mbura Muhindo[RIP]. He started as a member of the Uganda Patriotic Movement just like all young people were. He later crossed into the DP because the politics turned sectarian when the people of Busongora demanded that they need a candidate born in their county to represent them. They said they were tired of being represented by people from Bwera. In fact Bwera provided the most educated persons in the district just because the only junior secondary school was in Bwera. At this time the constituency of Kasese North was all out for grabs. The UPM had a candidate there who was form Bwera, Dr. Chrispus Kiyonga; the DP were planning to field Mr. Victor Bwambale who came from Mundongo Bwera, and the only educated person born in Kasese North was Jorome Mbura Muhindo who was at this time a known member of UPM. So there was tremendous confusion in this constituency.

The Democratic Party demanded that the party executive in Kasese send their candidates names to Mr. Bwengye in Bushenyi. Bwengye was the DP secretary general. A delegation of DP members left Kasese at night to meet with Bwengye in order to explain to the DP secretariat the dilemma they were facing at nomination. The DP local executive wanted to field Dr. Henry Bwambale in Bwera against UPC's Amon Bazira. They wanted to field Victor Muhindo in Kasese North against UPC's Adam Kisughu. The DP delegation was comprised of Mr. Ngelese of Bwera, Mr. Constantine Syauswa of Bwera and none from Busongora. The local Kasese north people wanted their own Mbura Muhindo to be the candidate and convinced him to cross from the UPM and join DP because it was the stronger party plus since he was a catholic, the voters would readily accept him. In fact Kasese had grown staunchly catholic and violently anti UPC. This now left Kiyonga without opposition in his own UPM party. He was therefore returned unopposed in the primaries in Kasese North. The struggle for the leadership of the DP in Kasese North escalated when the indigenous Basongora people forwarded the name of Mbura Muhindo to the DP secretariat. Unfortunately Francis Bwengye did not accept this nomination because he was aware that Mbura had just crossed from UPM and would not attract votes as Democratic Party candidate. Meanwhile as the struggle for leadership was raging on, the UPC had their own struggles in the same constituency. Kasese town had a person from Lango who vied for the seat in Kasese North as UPC candidate. His name was Mr. Patrick Olugo. He was generally supported by the non Bakonzo in the town. He was sure poised to win. This did not happen because the Rwenzururu movement did not allow primaries in the UPC. They had three appointed candidates and that was final. We were only going to face the candidates from other parties. Mr. Olugo then consented to become only the UPC chairman and was deputized by Christopher Balyebuga. A meeting was quickly held again in the Saad hotel on the eve of the nominations. Patrick Olugo assured the Rwenzururu delegation of his support for Adam Kisughu and encouraged his youth wingers to support the candidature of Adam Musa Kisughu. While we were in that meeting, Mr. Hasan Katigiti brought a note in the meeting. The note read that the DP delegation had returned from Bushenyi and Mr. Victor Muhindo had been confirmed as the DP candidate for Kasese North. We expected that the weaker and indigenous candidate, Mr. Mbura Muhindo would be recommended. This did not please Mr. Patrick Olugo. He instructed his youth wingers to arrest the DP candidate, lock him up in Rukoki until nominations were over. Mr. Paul Rwibende, the saza chief would be in charge of this operation to ensure that the DP candidate was released after the nomination closed. Mr. Patrick Olugo with his youth wingers came down from the meeting.

He left Amon Bazira, Blasio Maate, the Rwenzururu delegation and myself still in the meeting trying to lay a strategy about the nomination which was to happen the following morning. Early in the morning when Patrick Olugo came down by the hotel he found Mr. Victor Muhindo having a meal with Mrs. Henry Bwambale. Patrick Olugo sat in the hotel eating area a few tables away from Victor. Victor Bwambale was an assistant District Commissioner in Rukungiri District and he did not know who Olugo was, and what role he played in the politics of Kasese Township. The youth picked Mr. Victor; using a high jacked pickup truck, took him away while Olugo watched. When we asked Patrick Olugo what it had happened, he told us that the Democratic Party candidate had been taken to Rukoki. This was the morning of nomination.

The district commissioner having been delayed in the meeting for at least two hours did not start the process on time as had been stipulated by law. His office was supposed to open at 9:00am but did not open until 10:30 am. Rwenzururu leaders indirectly held the District Commisioner Mr. Blasio Maate hostage for two hours. During this time they were giving him instructions to make sure that he nominates the UPC members first before any other candidate.

Each candidate was supposed to come in with at least 9 people nominating them. These people were supposed to sign nomination papers before the process was completed. Nomination was allowed within three hours from the start of nomination. At this point the process was in the hands of the district commissioner, also called the returning officer. He did not know what had happened to the DP candidates. By 9:30am the UPC candidates had assembled at the District commissioner's office ready for nomination. The UPM candidate, Dr. Kiyonga was present with his team ready for nomination. The Democratic Party was still confused as to who was going to be nominated. Two names had been submitted to the Party secretariat in Bushenyi. However, one of the named candidates Mr. Victor Mihindo was missing. Confusion arose as Mbura Muhindo arrived with his team with members ready to nominate him while the members who had come to nominate Victor were also around the office. Dr. Henry Bwambale, Mr.Peter Kato and other members of the Democratic party were still working out a strategy of preventing Jerome Mburamuhindo from being nominated, but did not know that even their dream candidate was miss. The office was crowded by lots of onlookers. Before Mr. Maate could open his office, a group of DP supporters arrived in Peugeot station wagon looking for Mr. Steven Baluku. Noticeable among this gang was a Mr. Matovu, a Kawoya and Ngelese. They demanded to arrest Steven so that he takes them where Victor Muhindo had been taken. When I saw this confusion, I quickly commandeered a salon car that belonged to the driving school. I told him to drop me down town on Speke Street where Bazira was having last minute briefs with his supported as they had traveled all the way from Bwera to nominate him. When I arrived on Speke Street, I informed Bazira of the commotion that was happening at the DC's office. We quickly jumbed in Bazira's 120Y Datsun yellow in color Reg. UWR 150. As soon as we arrived at the office, the crowd had increased and Steven Baluku was being dragged in the station wagon. Because he was tall giant with some military training, they did not manage to squeeze him in the rear door as he was resisting furiously. Bazira, the former Director General of intelligence jumped out of his car, pulled out his private pistol and as soon as Matovu and Kawoya saw the "big man" with a pistol, they let go of Steven He had lost all the buttons of his shirt during the struggle. Bazira tried to move towards the office, and one Mr. Ngelese confronted him and asked him whether he know where they had taken Victor, because he was due for nomination. Bazira ignored him and moved on fast to try and disperse the crowd. His pistol fell from his hands, then he picked it and stuffed it back around his waist below his jacket. He really showed off his power as a former head of a security service this was the first time people saw his pistol in public. He did not return to Speke street. His supporters were already at the office, ready to nominate him. At this time, the DC opened his office and Bazira was the first to get in. Just in time. He was dully nominated. I was the second to squeeze in. There was such a struggle because we were all chasing time. It was first come, first served. I was dully nominated. As I was getting out, Dr. Kiyonga was right on the door with his supporters and he too was dully nominated. After Kiyonga' nomination, Adam Musa got in and was barely nominated as there was no more time left. In fact the district commissioner would have said no to Adam, but this was a Rwenzururu candidate. By the time the DC was done with Adam, it was way beyond the legal time for nominations. Dr. Henry Bwambale showed up late because he had been informed by his supporters that there was trouble at the DC's office and that one of the candidates of the DP was missing. Since he was the chairman of the district he was trying to sort things out by getting a substitute in place. However, as he arrived, Mr. Mbura Muhindo was standing outside the office, and frustrated that he could not make the time even when he was right there watching every candidate get nominated. One thing to note here was that the DP district executive did not endorse a UPM convert to stand on the DP ticket. They were struggling to find another alternative to Victor should he not show up for nomination. The bad news was that indeed he did not show up. Instead of taking him to Rukoki County headquarter to be in custody of Paul Rwibende, the Kasese north youth wingers took him to Kichwamba so that he does not find easy transport back in time for nomination. It is believed that some unknown people held him there. He was released late at night and we were informed that he could not find his way to the main road to Kasese. He stumbled into the Toro side of the boarder, and while he was asking for directions he spoke in Rutoro language because he knew he was on the Toro side of the boarder. Some Rwenzururu solders who were guarding the boarder found him and he spoke to them in Rutoro. It was understood that those soldiers stubbed him like they did to many Batoro people and buried him in a shallow grave. The next day we were informed that Victor had been found dead; his body was exhumed and taken to his home village in Mundongo, Bwera. The bitterness that followed here was un imaginable. To make matters even worse, no member of the Democratic Party was nominated, which meant that they would not field any candidates for the elections. This brought heavy resentment among the entire population. As a protest vote, the entire district vowed to vote for the Uganda Patriotic movement because this was the innocent party in this affair.

In Kasese south the DP candidate was Mr.Peter Kato, he was at the office, but because of confusion that had erupted, he too could not beat the clock. This then meant that Kasese south and Kasese West had returned their candidates unopposed. The real election then was in Kasese north. We had Adam for UPC and Chrispus for the UPM. As I mentioned, a protest vote was eminent. There was massive rigging by members of the DP who stole votes for UPM. Many UPC voters were intimidated that Mr. Adam at certain polling stations, polled 10 votes while UPM had polled over 1,000 votes. This happened in ridings which did not even have the population that warranted the votes collected.

As a final result, Dr. Chrispus Kiyonga was elected member of Kasese North constituency, although he too came from Bwera. Dr. Henry Bwambale filed a law suit against the Uganda Peoples' Congress. He filled his suit on behalf of the entire district, but the case was thrown out because he needed to file on behalf of his constituency not the district. He lost on technicalities.

Elections were held on December 10, 1980 and after Christmas it was time for us to go to the capital city Kampala to be sworn in as Members of Parliament.

In January, I met with Hon. Chrispus Kiyonga elect, discussed with him the strategy of developing our district. He was not happy the way Rwenzururu interfered in the politics of the district. We discussed with him the development of the town ship, I remember he collected and shared with me some statistics from the town clerk office regarding taxation in the general market. We debated about how much money the market collects in revenue for the town and how that money would be used to develop the town centre. This was truly the way forward for two members of parliament planning together matter of development. Kiyonga had been my mentor at one point when he was at Makerere university he kept on encouraging me to pursue higher school certificate and at one point promised that he would make it a point that he helped me get admitted into the faculty of Commerce at Makerere University. Although he was in the medical faculty, he promised that with my combination of HEG, [history, economics and Geography] he would use his influence on campus to get me admitted. We again met with Dr. Kiyonga in February in Kampala when I was preparing to go for swearing in. I met him on Kampala road near Uganda House, which hosted the headquarters of UPC; asked him whether he was considering coming to parliament for the swearing in ceremony. He was very adamant about this. At one point he told me he was not interested in joining a parliament where he was the only member of a political party. His own party leader Mr. Kaguta Museveni had lost to Mr. Kutesa a member of the Democratic Party. In March of 1981 the leader of the UPM party went to the bush to fight the elected government. After the swearing ceremony in February I moved to Kasese to start a crusade that would see an explosion in education.

CHAPTER 12

Education: the prerequisite for Development

1981 was the year in which the Kasese leaders would sit down together regardless of their party affiliations to discuss the causes of the district's backwardness. As a former teacher it was incumbent upon me to organize the local leaders, the civic leaders and the politicians to constitute ourselves into a committee to look into the history of education in our area. On one occasion, We invited the Minister of Education Prof. Isaac Ojok and the Minister of Transport and communication, Mr. Mugenyi. They travelled by train from Kampala to Kasese. We wanted the Minster of Transport to have a feel of the train as it was the gateway to Education for this district and we brought the minister of education with him to discuss improvement and upgrade to Saad secondary school. Mr. Enoch and the two members of parliament from Kasese as well as the district commission at the time Mr. Senyonga standing in for Mr. Maate received the ministers at Saad secondary school as seen in picture.

In 1976 Amin Dada allowed the Moslems from Mpodwe to open the first Secdondary School. It started from the premises of Kisinga primary school. After two years, the school moved to its present location at Kiburara. The sole financier of the school was Magdad Saad, with money left by his late father Hajji Saad. By the time Amin fell, the school was still a private school. In 1979 when during Binaisa's rule, Bazira and Henry Bwambale met with the minister of Education secured government aided status for the school. A school lorry was also secured. This was the only secondary school in the area.

When we met as leaders, we resolved to promote education by opening up more secondary schools and expanding the existing primary schools. When Mr. Adam Musa failed to make it to parliament, he resumed his old job as district education officer. We worked together to open and upgrade the existing primary schools. In 1981 I held a meeting at Kyarumba trading center and called upon business men to donate their money towards opening a secondary school in that area. After that meeting one businessman by the name of Ezroni Syajjabbi volunteered to donate 5,000/-. This was what was needed to show to the ministry of education that you were capable of operation a private school. I went with this man to Kampala and met with the minister of Education Prof. Isaac Newton Ojok. At this time I explained to the minister the injustice that had happened to the district. I explained the recent history and the willingness of the Rwenzururu movement to assist in making sure that the schools we were about to open would be secure. The minister did not only grant private school status, he actually approved partial government assistance. This was the birth of Mutwanywana Secondary School. This now brought the number of secondary schools to two. In the same year 1981 the District education officer Mr. Adam led a delegation to Kampala to see the Minister. They demanded that a secondary school be opened in Kasese north constituency. The minister agreed to have Rwenzori High opened as a government school. So within one year in political office we had a secondary school to each constituency. These schools were purely parents initiated with guidance from the members of parliament. The following year, 1982 the parents of Bwera sub county met with their Member of parliament Mr. Amon Bazira and expressed the wish to have a secondary school in their area. They argued that if Kyarumba, which was considered a land locked village [cupboard] can open a secondary school, why wouldn't Bwera do the same? The MP relented and met with the Minister of Education to explain the need for an additional secondary school. At this time we did not even have enough teachers to run these schools. The only school that had been around for some time was Saad Secondary school. We were therefore depleting the oldest school of qualified teachers. We had already convinced Mr. Lazarus Muhindo to leave Saad where he was the science teacher to come to Kyarumba and head Mutanywana Secondary school. When Rwenzori High school opened, Mr. Mbayahi Jethro had just finished his degree in Education from the University of Nairobi. He became an easy target to spot for Rwenzori high school. In 1982 when Bwera opened we had to fish again from Saad secondary and **removed** Mrs. Loice Bwambale to come and head the school. She later left the school to become the first Woman to represent Kasese in the National parliament. Fearless as she was, many critics referred to her as the "Kasese iron lady" because she withstood the pressures of men who wanted to unseat her.

Ours was just a crash program; we did not care whether only the Headmaster would be the qualified teacher. We were just after having secondary schools in place and the rest would take care of themselves as the situations dictated. In 1983 the parents of Karambi called for a meeting with their Member of Parliament. He was not available at this time because he was on an overseas trip to Iraq. He authorized me to meet with his constituents on his behalf. I went to Karambi. During this meeting, the hot topic was a need for a secondary school in Karambi Sub County. I said yes, to the idea and I arranged a meeting with the chairman of the parents association. We went and met the minister of Education and requested for a secondary school. It was granted on partial government aid. Right then we looked for a Karambi graduate to head the school. We landed on Mbusa Joseph with whom I had been to college. Mbusa was not the most qualified for the job but he had exceptional leadership qualities and was capable of heading a secondary school. By end of 1983 we had 5 secondary schools. The opposition leaders heavily criticized us. They said we are opening secondary school on the primary schools premises, they also said we did not have qualified teachers to run the school. We decided to ignore their criticisms, as this would deter us from opening more school. One thing we saw as a positive was each time we opened a school around a primary school premises, there was immediate expansion as the parents worked hard to put up extra buildings to replace those used by the secondary school. Our primary target was that if by 1984 we had at least five secondary school, we would have 200 students sitting for their O'level exams. This would be for sure 100% Bakonzo kids. And this was the plain truth as we offered no apologies for this percentage. It had never happened before for our district to have 200 kids sitting for their senior four exams. It is at this time that I would like to acknowledge with gratitude the efforts put in by the teachers who were hired to execute this plan. All the teachers who worked hard during this time deserve to be acknowledged for the tireless effort they put in to educate these young Bakonzo kids during difficult educational circumstances. I know some have passed on like the late Lazaro Muhindo RIP and Jerome Mburamuhindo, while others have left teaching to take on political responsibilities, but we should congratulate them as well. In 1984 I visited the permanent secretary in the ministry of education to negotiate for at least two schools to offer higher school certificate. During this year we had invited the Ministers of Education both Hon. Philemon Mateke and Prof. Isaac Ojok had visited the district and were impressed at what we had achieved in a span of three years. They had presided over fundraising functions at Mutaywana Secondry School, Saad Secondary school and Bwera Secondary school. At one point we had invited the Prime Minister the Hon. Otema Alimadi to come to Kasese. During his visit he attended fundraising functions at Kagando hospital and later traveled to Rwenzori high school. We had invited in as many cabinet ministers as we could and the message had been received with surprise to see that we were only having our first secondary schools since independence. So when I requested for two schools to offer high school certificate, I readily got the correct answer. In 1984 Mutanywana secondary school opened an Arts class for senior five. Saad Secondary school as well was allowed to open senior 5 arts class. The reasoning was if we were going to have at least 200 students sitting for their O'levels, we will have some students who will not be admitted in senior 5 in those 'prestigious' well established school. We thought that if we had our own schools offering high school certificate, at least out of 200 we might conservatively have 50 joining high school certificate classes while others with lower grades might be admitted in other post secondary institutions. And if 50 joined senior five, at least by the end of the two years, we would have perhaps 25 students making it to the University. As the trend was in the past we always had a few who were admitted to other schools especially in boarding school, We could probably have another 10 – 15 students from these schools being admitted to the University. So the hope was at least by 1986 we would have at least 30 - 40 students from Kasese being admitted to Makerere University. This number would increase every year as the facilities and the quality of teaching improved. I did not stay in the country to see this happen but statistics will show that from 1986 the explosion into education was evident and the celebration of this literacy has resulted into quality manpower in the district. The year 1984 was the year many activities happened around education. In 1983 Parliament nominated me to join a group of 3 other MPs to attend an inter- parliamentary conference in the city of Geneva, Switzerland. While there I met with an American senator and a Canadian Member of Parliament. I discussed with them the strategy we were using to improve education in our area. They shared with me their own experiences before they received their freedom from the British. They told me about their aboriginal people who were discriminated in their own land by settlers but now were also fighting for their rights to education, health care and economic independence. During this discussion I realized that the Bakonzo had gotten similar experiences, as they were being ruled by the Batoro. My conclusion after meeting with these honorable and experienced legislators was that there was need to engage the government, dialogue with positive presentations and involve the local people in decision-making. When I returned I held a meeting with the speaker of parliament to give him a feed back from my trip and to discuss an invitation that was extended to me by the US senator. The speaker, Hon. Francis Butagira plainly told me that parliament did not have enough money to sponsor my trip to the United States. I moved on with my development plans. In that same year I decided to have a meeting with the citizens of Lake Katwe. I introduced the idea of a technical college to them. I asked them to think about it and report to me within two weeks. After two weeks I went to Lake Katwe and met the local Uganda People Congress chairman, Mr. Bisanku RIP, together with our Constituency UPC secretary Mr. Christopher Katemba. They had organized a large gathering like a town hall meeting. We brain stormed ideas about a technical school. We discussed the benefits of such a school, both to our children and to the community. At this meeting we agreed that we occupy the abandoned building of Kabatoro, which belonged to the town council. I now had the backing of the parents and the business people of Katwe; I had involved the people in making a decision that would affect their community. I went to the Ministry of Education and requested for a technical institution. I explained to the minister that we were going to have many students who will not make it to higher school certificate. Out of the 200 students who would be sitting for O'levels, if 50 went to HSC, we would have more than 100 who would qualify for vocational schools. Since Kasese did not have any, I convinced the minister that it was a prudent move to have at least one technical school. In the same gesture, the Member of Parliament for Kasese West Hon. Amon Bazira was pursuing the same strategy and advocated for a teachers' college, which would take again some of the remnants from the 200 students. We were trying to make sure that we fit every student in some kind of institution. In 1984 the DEO [district Education officer] reported that intake in primary school had soared so high that he did not have enough teachers to meet the upsurge. It was like the parents suddenly woke up and sent their children to school. The only Teachers' training College had just started and was not ready to produce teachers yet. The existing teachers were mostly grade two and the standards were getting higher and higher.

At this time I thought of opening another institution, which would produce teachers quicker. A teachers' College that trained grade two teachers and upgraded them to grade three was what we needed. This program took only one year. Pragmatically, I went to Rwenzori High school, pulled out Mr. Mbayahi and went with him to Kampala. He did not know why I invited him to go with me to Kampala. We went discussing the possibility of opening up a grade three teachers' college. At first he thought Bwera Teachers College was enough, but I told him, that to go to Bwera Teachers college, you had to first pass O'level and stay at college for two year before you could come out and teach. The new teachers' College would admit already qualified teachers, and would offer upgrade courses. That way we would have within one year a bunch of qualified grade three teachers. Mr. Mbayahi saw the point. I went with him to see the permanent secretary to the ministry of education. I told him that I need a license to operate a grade three teachers college which would only admit grade two teachers who wanted to upgrade. I informed the Permanent Secretary that I already had a principal in the name of Jethro Mbayahi. He was right there with me. The permanent secretary Mr. Latigo had no choice than to grant the license, because he saw how serious I was and how urgent the need for qualified teachers was; knowing the history we had just gone through as a tribe.

On that day Jethro Mbayahi was appointed the principal of Kinyamaseke Teachers' College. He then came and sat with the parents of Kinyamaseke primary school to negotiate to use their buildings while helping to build some for the primary school. Mr. Zephania Bwambale was the chairman of the parents committee at the same time he was the vice chairman of the UPC constituency executive committee. So the ideas fell on fertile ground, it was like filling gaps in a puzzle with the right people in place. Each individual we spotted and placed in a school cooperated and worked to the best of their ability. They all understood our recent history and were willing to do what they could to contribute to the success of the process. Mr. Enoch Muhindo was a lecturer at the Kyambogo Teachers' University College; he volunteered to quit that job and come to head Saad Secondary school to bring it to standard, because it now offered A-Level courses. A newly graduated Muranga was to replace Mbayahi at Ruwenzori High school and a technician from Kilembe Mr. Turyagenda was to head the Katwe Technical School. He was not a teacher by profession, but because we could not find a teacher qualified in the technical field we just went in the Kilembe mines and found one who was willing to use his practical experience to pass on technical knowledge. He was a Mukiga by tribe. It was his responsibility to look for other teacher to help him produce successful students in the technical fields. During the same year1982, Kasese North constituency was undergoing a bi election to replace Dr. Kiyonga who had left the country. The constituency was all up for grabs again. Mr. Steven Baluku, Mr. Adam Musa, Mr. Bruno Bwambale and Lt. Tom Baluku were all vying for the same seat and were all belonging to the same party.

At that time I was the Chairman of the district. The District seat was a rotational seat, and in 1982 the chairman of Kasese South was the chairman of the district. I was therefore to manage the primary elections. Mr. Amon Bazira put his weight around Mr. Bruno Bwambale because he had just convinced him to abandon DP. The UPC secretariat put their weight on Lt. Tom Baluku. They even sent a campaigner Mr. Lobidra to come and help Tom win the Kasese north seat. Mr. Steven Baluku and Adam Musa were on their own. I was the neutral figure in this election as the chairman. I probably would have wanted Adam Musa because he kept the flame of the party going and helped in the development of the projects we had started. But I left it for the people to decide.

At the primaries, Tom Baluku prevailed and Adam was just the runners up. Steven and Bruno both combined their votes and gave them to Adam, but still he lost to the Lt. Tom Baluku. So in 1983 Kasese north had a member of parliament. We now had our UPC team complete. I sat with Tom Baluku in his Kasese north parliamentary office and we discussed the possibility of starting another secondary school in Kilembe. My argument was that all the schools we had started were in areas where there was no electricity; therefore, they would confine themselves to Arts subjects.

I proposed to the MP that we arrange a meeting with the management of Kilembe mines and ask them to offer some of their buildings in Kyajuki which we could transform into classrooms. I was hoping that since there was electricity here, we would open a school that would offer science subjects that required electricity. We visited Kilembe mines and held a meeting with the general manager Mr. Mulindwa and explained to him why we need buildings in Kyajuki for a secondary school. Mr. Mulindwa and his personnel manager Mr. Onyango were positive and promised that they would provide the premises, restructure them to suit classroom environment and would also help to provide furniture for both classes and staff house. To me this was going to be *"the school"*. After this meeting, I went to my office in Kasese, put an announcement on radio Uganda requesting a Mr. George Bazirakakye to come to Kasese to meet with me. He did not have a clue as to why he was being called to come to Kasese. He had never been to Kasese. He was a teacher at Kigezi high school as head of the science department. We knew each other since I had been a teacher there in 1979. So George came to Kasese to meet with an old colleague who had become a member of parliament. Within three days, I saw Mr. Bazirakakye arriving at my office by bus from Kabale. I took him to my residence in Kilembe. I called the Member of Parliament, Lt. Tom Baluku to my house and we discussed the possibility of having George head the secondary school in Kilembe. This was great news to him, as he accepted the offer. We then traveled to Kampala to meet with the ministry of education. Lt. Tom Baluku and I met with Prof. Isaac Ojok and explained why we needed a secondary school in Kilembe. We discussed the importance of a school that would offer science subjects because of the facilities for laboratory equipment, which other schools could not afford. The minister of education accepted our request, ordered his Permanent secretary to appoint George Bazirakakye as the headmaster with immediate effect. Mbura Muhindo had been appointed Headmaster of Kasese secondary school which started in 1982 without political initiative. This was purely a parents initiated school..

So by the end of 1984 Kasese District boasted of having 7 secondary school, 2 teacher training colleges, and 1 Technical institute at Katwe. All these were government-sponsored institutions. Kichwamba secondary school and Kitolhu secondary school were the only private schools at the time. 1985 was going to be the election year. Dr. Obote ordered that each constituency in the country be allocated one million Uganda shillings as a development fund. This was the money that was going to start up the campaigns against the Democratic Party. As for Kasese, we were for sure going to win, because we had proved to the population that we were capable of keeping our promises and we could deliver during the second term in office. We had been able to pull the district from one secondary school to ten [10] post primary institutions. The number of primary schools had increased as well. The second term was going to be devoted to clean water projects, Health centre and hospitals, good roads and other social services that were necessary for a developing district. Kasese West was already earmarked for a hospital, which was to supliment Kagando, and Kilembe. These two were the only private Hospitals serving a population of over 700,000 people. Peace had returned to the district by the discending of the Rwenzururu leadership in 1982. Uganda Poeples Congress had transformed the district with dianamic leadership.

CHAPTER 13

Politics and the church: Kasese was no exception

The church in Kasese underwent tremendous changes in 1979 when the entire district was governed by the Rwenzururu authorities. The hard hit religion with this change of political and civil authority was the Anglican Church. During Christmas of 1979 and that of 1980 the Irema Ngoma leadership ordered that all gift collections; tithing and donations should not be given to the diocese headquarters in Fort Portal as was the practice. Instead he ordered that all collections be handed to the "ministry" responsible for church under the Rwenzururu leadership. Any church that would not comply would face severe punishment. So the pastors and church leaders had to comply. Some of the reverends who were kicked out of Toro during the exodus had been assigned to head small churches. The Rwenzururu leadership demanded that the church of Uganda authorize the church in Kasese to govern itself in a new and separate diocese from that of Rwenzori, which was governed by Fort Portal. In 1981 Bishop Rwakaikara retired. He was allowed to come and preach his fare well sermons to the Kasese churches on condition that he will not demand for the money collected during Christmas of 1980 to be taken to Fort Portal. The new elected

Bishop was Bishop Kamanyire. During his consecration speech, he called the Rwenzururu leaders "rebels" and he appealed to them to surrender the money they withheld so that he can run the affairs of the diocese well. In turn, the Rwenzururu leaders banned him from ministering to churches in Kasese. They said he would be arrested if he dared visit Kasese. Amon Bazira and I attending his consecration ceremony held at the cathedral in Kabarole. Bishop Kamanyire later appointed me to be his representative on the Diocesan synod representing the churches from Kasese. When we realized that the Rwenzururu leadership would not relent, we invited the Arch Bishop of Uganda Rt. Rev.Silvanas Wani. We arranged a meeting between Irema Ngoma and the Arch Bishop. The meeting took place at the Historic Nsenyi catholic parish. The Bishop of Rwenzori Dioces, Rev. Kamanyire, accompanied Arch Bishop Wani, members of his privy council accompanied Irema Ngoma and on the government side we had the District commissioner Mr. Blasio Maate. On the political side we had Amon Bazira the MP for Kasese west and Myself as the MP for Kasese south. Canon Steven Mukirane and Ven. Yona Kule represented the local church. At the meeting the Rwenzururu delegation emphatically told the arch Bishop that Kasese demanded for a separate diocese. The archbishop responded that a separate diocese would not be achieved by confiscating the money that was meant to run the church. At this time the pastors in Kasese had gone several months without salaries and most churches were surviving by the mercy of the Lord. The Arch bishop and the Irema Ngoma struck a deal. Bishop Yonasani Kamanyire was allowed to come and preach in Kasese to prepare the Christians for a separate diocese and the Rwenzururu leaders agreed to release the money in order to pay for the salaries of the Kasese reverends and church leaders. Irema Ngoma demanded that a second arch deaconry be established to create room for priests who were kicked out of Fort portal. Among them was the Venerable Yona Kule who was dean of the Cathedral in Fort Portal and principal of Bukuku theological college. The archbishop agreed to create a second arch deaconry to create a job for Rev. Yona Kule. At this time Steven Mukirane became the arch deacon of Kisinga while Yona Kule became the arch deacon of Kasese. A committee

97

was set in place to continue discussions and negotiations to bring to reality the establishment of a separate Diocese. Mr. Muhyana was nominated chairman of such committee comprised of the two arch Deacons, Steven and Yona plus a few Christians from the Bwera church. A committee of three was formed to draft a constitution; the members were Amos Kambere, Ivan Muhasa and the church lawyer Mr. Nyakana of Fort Portal. As a representative of Bishop Kamanyire on the Diocesan synod, I was charged with representing the views of the Arch Deaconry of Kasese and Kisinga in the synod. I did not even sit on this synod because it did not take long before we got our own diocese. At this time as was always the case like other positions in the district, we did not have anyone qualified to head the diocese. One native Pastor from Kasese was in the united stated studying. His name was Rev. Zebedee Masereka, an old boy of mine from the National Teachers' College of Kyambogo. Rev. Z. Masereka had graduated from Kyambogo University College, and went off to Nyakasura to become the chaplain for the school. It was from here that he left for the United States on church scholarship to study divinity. He already had a diploma in education, a diploma in theology and was now admitted into a USA theological college where he graduated with a Masters Degree in Divinity. He came back to be the Dean of the Kabarole Cathedral. By the end of 1982 Bishop Kamanyire had concluded his pastoral visit in Kasese and declared that we were ready for our own diocese.

The stories he received and the reports he got from the priests convinced him that he could not insist on keeping Kasese under the Rwenzori diocese. We now had to go through a process of selecting a Bishop to head the upcoming diocese.

The province in Kampala had heard from Arch Bishop Wani and the recommendation was that Kasese be granted a separate diocese from Kabarole. The business of selecting a Bishop was left to Bishop Kamanyire's synod. This became my first and last synod meeting to attend. At this synod meeting I was appointed the chairman of the Electoral College. I was therefore to take my seat not as a voter from the Kasese arch deaconry, but as a chairman to over see the election of a new diocese. The new diocese was to be called South Rwenzori diocese because we already had the catholic diocese called Kasese Diocese headquartered in Bunyaruguru. Every archdeaconry was allowed constitutionally to send 9 representatives who would participate in the election. So because Kasese had only two archdeaconries, we had 18 delegates. The rest of the delegates from other arch deaconry of the Rwenzori diocese were to participate in the election. In other wards even delegates from Bwamba, Burahya and Bunyangabo arch deaconries participated in electing a Bishop for the new diocese of South Rwenzori. As the chairman of the Electoral College, I did not have the chance to cast my vote, I carried my vote with me as a souvenir. We had three candidates who contested for the job of Bishop. They were Rev. Yona Kule, Rev. Steven Mukirane and Rev. Zebedee Masereka. Only one of the three was really qualified to head a diocese. I conducted the elections in a free and fair fashion. At the end of the day, the Very Rev. Zebedee Kahangwa Masereka was returned as the Bishop of South Rwenzori diocese. I passed the results of the vote to the Bishop and the process of establishing a new diocese started. We then left Fort Portal to go and start the preparations of consecrating a new Bishop. Amon Bazira used his business contacts in Kampala to secure for the diocese a new car for the bishop. A small Hyndai light green in color was secured on loan to be paid for by the money that was being held by the Rwenzururu leaders. We negotiated with Kilembe mines to allow the Bishop to live in their quarters at McGowan. We moved to Kampala as a team of three members of parliament to invite the President to be present at what was to be a historic moment in the history of the people of Kasese. Two years prior to this, Irema Ngoma had come down with his entire army and now August 15, 1984 H.E. the President Dr. Obote would accept our invitation to attend this function, which would be officiated by the Arch Bishop of Uganda, the RT. Rev. Yona Okoth. All the bishops of the church of Uganda attended the function.

I do not think Kasese district will ever have political leaders who will be as busy and involved as we were between 1981 and 1985. We dealt with critical and sensitive issues at the same time keeping the people united and peaceful. There was no evidence of

99

massive loss of life or property during this time. At the same time we do not condone the loss of a few during the early years of our term of office. The district lost Victor Muhindo, Patric Olugo and Edward Sempebwa under unexplained circumstances; all three were of significant importance. While we moarned these lives, we kept the people united, progressive and productive.

CHAPTER 14

Rwenzururu: The final episode

Amon Bazira and I had been involved right from the time Kasese fell to the Rwenzururu Movement after Idi Amin. A relationship was created during the time we were negotiating with the 'king', first to stop the taxation that had been going on for years and second to surrender the church money that had been confiscated during the Christmas of 1979 and 80. We held several meetings with the 'King's Privy Council' and the King Irema Ngoma himself. Bazira was not very fluent in Lukonzo, and one of the words that used to give him hard time and created good humor amongst the kings entourage was; "emitheghekere". He used to pronounce it the way a mutoro would say it. And whenever he said words like "emitheghekere ya banyabuthoki" there was laughter all the time lending humour to the discussion. I was the fluent guy and did most of the talking. Bazira always came prepared with money because one of the demands that was put on the table when Bazira convinced them to abandon the taxation policy, they said; "how do we pay the soldiers, members of the privy council and ministers?" Bazira always gave them huge sums of Uganda shillings. He did not tell me how much it was each time, but I could see it was a lot of money. They were happy, because they had money to replace whatever they had been collecting from people.

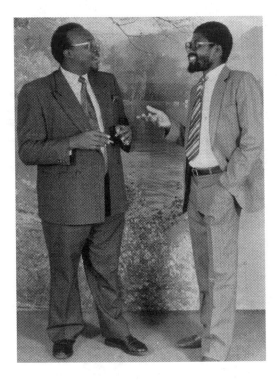

We also convinced them to stop collecting "unga" from citizens. It had been common practice for them to collect cassava flour from every village to feed the Rwenzururu soldiers. Again as we gave them some money, they accepted to stop this practice. On each market day, every fish monger was to submit at least 2 tilapia fish to chiefs because the Rwenzururu leaders wanted to feed well. Again this was a practice we brought to an end. There were so many things the movement was doing which were displeasing to their own people. These had to stop. We made sure that we closed every avenue in which they squeezed the common man. That is why when you talk of the UPC leadership of the 1980s, people will remember the agony that was removed from them by eliminating the unnecessary suffering that was a common practice by Rwenzururu soldiers. Amon Bazira and Amos Kambere as pictured above are credited for stopping those encumberances.

After the meeting at the historic Nsenyi parish with the Archbishop, we organized another meeting to strike a major deal for the King to descend from the mountains and relinquish his authority to the central government. In 1981 we made several trips to Kalingwe and Kahindangoma to meet with Charles Wesley Irema Ngoma. At each of these meetings we had the district commissioner Mr. Maate with us as a symbol and gesture of how the government was seriously interested in negotiating with the Rwenzururu movement. Dr. Obote had given us the mandate to negotiate on behalf of the government. Before we left parliamentary buildings we told Milton Obote that the first UPC government lost lots of money, lives and property. They did not succeed in eliminating the movement. We further reiterated that Amin with his mighty army, even after giving them the district, did not eliminate them, instead more lives were lost and more money was spent on the army trying to fight a civil rebellion that could have been solved by negotiations. So on our part we had convinced the government that peace talks and a message of reconciliation was the way forward. Before we moved on our final approach, we first agreed among ourselves what we would accept if we were in their shoes. We did some role play here, and one of us pretended to be the 'king". We knew that these people had fought a bitter war for twenty years, and it was time for them to give it up. So we started with what we would need if we were in their shoes as we came down for the first time? First we suggested a **house** to live in. Second we thought of a **car** to travel, Third, we thought of how he would **earn a living**, and next what would the future be like, and finally what title would the king have after stripping him of his "rebel royal" titles. We also asked what would happen to the many soldiers he had recruited into the Rwenzururu army. **So we suggested a house, a saloon car, a bus, a truck/Tata Lorry, a small pickup. In additioin we suggested two commercial buildings in Kasese town to generate income for the entire house hold.** After answering these questions, we moved on to climb to the furthest private cave at Kahindangoma. We put these suggestions on the table and asked the 'king' to discuss them with his cabinet. At first they kind of liked the proposals, but then they said these only took care of the King, what about the rest of the leaders, the fighters, etc?

We quickly came up with the answer. We suggested that the fighters would be absorbed into the national army, the UNLA and the rest of the 'ministers' would be appointed into local chiefs and other positions within the local government. At this meeting, we were just creating goodwill, we had to go back to our own government and convince the President that all the demands were worth the expenditure, because we would be solving a civil rebellion once and for all. The expenditure would not be equivalent to the loss of lives and property on both the side of the government soldiers and the civilian casualties plus the long existing conflict between the Bakonzo and Batooro which would come to an end. Dr. Milton Obote gave us the green light. He authorized us to arrange a meeting between his army chief of staff, his minister of state for security and the Irema Ngoma team. At this point we knew we were on the right truck and were about to strike the bull's eye. So we made our regular climb via Nsenyi parish, we met with Reverend Father Balinandi, the parish priest at the time. He agreed to host the meeting between the Uganda government officials and the officials of the Rwenzururu movement. We made our trek uphill and met with the king. We requested for a meeting in which they would have to put their demands on the table. We told them that the President of Uganda was willing to meet their demands as long as these would bring to end the civil rebellion and would enable the king to come and live among his people and talk about development and not destruction of lives and property. A day was set for the meeting. We had a compelling reason for the use of political incentives where the king's cabinet would be absorbed within the work force even though most of them might not have been qualified. We were determined to use negotiations and mediation tactics instead of coercion and punishment which had failed in the past. This conflict had deterred development of schools, roads and hospitals. The government was more concerned with quelling the civil rebellion than thinking about development. Conditions for development had to be created, and we were committed to bring this to a peaceful conclusion in order for us to push our agenda of development through the UPC government.

In early 1982 Major General David Oyite Ojok, Uganda's Chief of Staff, Hon. Chris Rwakasisi, Minister of State Office of the President responsible for security, made up the government delegation while the Irema Ngoma, Prime Minister Yeremia Muhongya and several members of the Privy Council made up the Rwenzururu delegation. The District Commissioner Kasese Mr. Maate, Hon. Bazira and Hon. Kambere represented the local leadership. The meeting was held amidst heavy security provided by the Rwenzururu soldiers. The first check point manned by Rwenzururu soldiers was at Kagando hospital. Every one who traveled from Kasese, including David Oyite Ojok's guards, was disarmed. All guns were held at that point. The second was at Kiswahili's house at Kisinga Trading center, and the third was 100 meters from the Nsenyi Parish church. The Uganda Army Chief of Staff saw how the roadways leading to Nsenyi parish were militarized by rebel soldiers in uniforms similar to that of the Ugandan Army.

At one time Rwakasisi whispered to Oyite Ojok that, "can you imagine, you the Nations Chief of Staff, disarmed? This means you have been stripped off your military authority, you are at their mercy," It sounded like treason and yet it was not. It looked like a movie story, and yet it was real. The situation was tense. At Nsenyi parish about 25 soldiers, heavily armed formed what we later knew was a guard of honour. Oyite Ojok was forced to ceremoniously inspect this guard of honour and when Irema Ngoma arrived, they sang the Rwenzururu anthem plus the Uganda National anthem. Irema Ngoma too inspected this guard of honour mounted by his own troops. After this, we went into the meeting room. The tension was relaxed when Rev. Father Balinandi opened with a word of prayer and the meeting started. Rwakasisi welcomed the king from his mountain hideout to the plains, delivered greetings from the president of Uganda. Oyite Ojok delivered greetings from the army commander, General Tito Okello, and promised to deploy the willing and able Rwenzururu soldiers into the national army.

Irema Ngoma on his part accepted the conditions we had laid on the table. He wanted reassurance from the government that what we had proposed to him would be a reality if he should accept to come down peacefully.

He promised to come down and join the government in the struggle of reconstruction and reconciliation.

So a day was set as August 15th 1982 when the king and his entire army plus their arms would descend the hills of Kahindangoma down to Nsenyi and then to Kasese boma ground. At the time we were going on with the negotiations, one of Irema Ngoma's brothers, William Sibibuka, had been held by the army in Mbarara and was being looked after by Lt. Tom Baluku who was assigned to the Western Brigade at Mbarara. Irema Ngoma requested that his brother be released unconditionally. The chief of staff David Oyite Ojok promised to look into this matter. He actually instructed Captain Namiti together with Tom Baluku to have William brought back to his family. It is from this connection that Lt. Tom Baluku came to be in contact with the King and the Rwenzururu establishment.

On the day of coming down, The District Commissioner and the members of parliament went to Nsenyi to welcome the king and his entire army. We took two lorries, plus one bus to transport the entire Rwenzururu army. That night, Irema Ngoma was smuggled by Lt. Tom Baluku assisted by Captain Namiti to spend the night in Mweya Safari Lodge. They managed to do this without the local leaders' knowledge as well as the Rwenzururu chief of staff. There was fear that Kinyamusitu who was the Rwenzururu chief of staff had refused to comply with the negotiated deal. He vowed to stay in the mountains and continue fighting. There was fear that he could harm the king by staging a palace coup; and that was why Tom and Namiti smuggled him into Mweya and delivered him very early in the morning to the foothills near Nsenyi to appear as if he was coming from up the mountains. So for the first time, in 20 years, Irema Ngoma first came to Mweya before he officially entered the Peugeot 505, which had been prepared to ferry him to the Boma ground in Kasese. On 15th August 1982 a long motorcade descended on Kasese boma grounds, carrying the "Bakonzo king" with majority of his arms and ammunitions. It was a day of jubilation as it marked the end of the 20 years of bitterness, the long years of suffering, backwardness, and insubordinations. This was the beginning of progress, the beginning of mature politics that looked at development and not destruction. The ceremony was attended by Uganda government ministers, members of parliament and an estimated 20,000 thousand people. People came from all neighboring districts, including the traditional enemies, Toro district. All to come and see the "king" who, for more than 20 years had defied arrest, kept the army on their feet and kept politicians and government leaders including presidents restless.

Charles Kisembo Iremangoma, king of Rw~~ ~~~'u addressing the public in Kasese Aug 15, 1982.

In a speech prepared for him him to read, Iremangoma had this to say, and I quote: "...We have come down, not as surrender, but to come and join the government, to work and find solutions to our people's problems..." In Rwenzururu 20 years of Bitterness, Bazira contends that, I quote: "***that, finding solutions to our problems had been the primary objectives of the Rwenzururu leadership.*** For example he mentions that "Isaya Mukirane believed that there was a sense of superior group position prevailing in Uganda where by some people thought that their tribes were better than the Bayira; a matter that resulted in the subordination of the Bayira and the low political esteem accorded them. He had come to the conclusion that in most cases discrimination was practiced against the Bayira covertly unknown to the victims and that a muyira in Uganda unlike a muyira in Congo begins the race of life with a detectable handicap of discrimination". [Bazira pp 12]. These are some of the issues Irema Ngoma referred to when he said he and his team had come down to work with the government to find solutions to and crash discrimination in all its forms. Some of the issues that were addressed as a result of this decision were notably the creation of a separate diocese for the people of Kasese. Negtotiations to have this effected were carried out between the former arc-bishop of Uganda the Most Rev. Salivanas Wani and the honorable members of parliament at the time; the then bishop of Rwenzori the Rev. Yonasani Kamanyire. Progessively after two years after Irema Ngoma came down, on August 15, 1984 the first Bishop of south Rwenzori diocese was installed. This accession was graced by the attendance of the president of Uganda at the time, Dr. Apolo Milton Obote.

CHAPTER 15

The 1985 coup d'état

It is 11:30 on July 27th 1985. A close friend of mine comes running to my office on Margarita Street in Kasese town. "The government has been overthrown" he reported. You must be kidding, I answered. He insisted and pulled out a transistor radio from his pocket. Here listen for yourself!! As I listen, I heard the voice of Lt. Ochora announcing that the government had been overthrown and that Brig. Bazirio Olara Okello was in charge. I thanked him for the information and it appeared that He was the only one who so far knew. I picked up my brief case, came slowly down the stairs, to the street. I saw the UPC chairman Mr. Balyebuga standing casually on the street in a leisurely conversation with Captain Otto. Looking at their body language I realize that they had not got the news of the take over. I did not want to tell them, because I did not know what the army officer would do, because he was from the Bazirio Okello tribe. I was with my constituency treasurer, I jumped into my red datsun car, took off for Kilembe. While driving to Kilembe I tuned on my car radio and indeed the government was gone, there was news that the President had fled the country and that the coup was bloodless. So I got to my house in Kilembe, my wife was pregnant with our second child. She had gone to Bwera to attend a wedding of our friend Constance Mutooro wedding Mika. I packed my brief case with some money plus a few clothes and wanted to head for Congo boarder immediately. What I feared mostly were the rebels of the NRA whom we had prevented from taking over Kasese and were still hanging around the hills of Bunyangabo and Maliba. We would be easy targets when they get in town.

I then jumped in my car and drove. I was hoping that I would just drive through and get to the boarder before things worsened. This did not happen. As I drove towards Kasese, I came across a convoy of vehicle all running towards Kilembe and every one I passed waved me to turn back. The indication was that the town was not safe to drive through. The news of the coup had now arrived home and every one was on the run. My treasurer and I made a complete U turn and headed back to Kilembe. When I got back to my house, I parked the car, went in the house to scribble a note to my wife that I was heading for Congo through the mountains. After the note, we started the long climb. When we reached the top of the mountain overlooking Kilembe, where we could still see my house, we stopped and tuned on the transistor radio. We saw NRA soldiers who were hiding among the population coming to my house. They did not loot any thing, but they entered my bedroom to remove the gun they knew I had. Rev. Mutazindwa himself came to my house to remove the gun. On the radio it was being announced that Bazirio Olara Okello was after Dr. Obote, Rwakasisi and Peter Otai. All other ministers were free. We did not take chance anyhow. We moved through the hills while monitoring Kampala via the transistor radio. On the second day of the coup, we heard the announcement of the head of state as being that of Gen. Tito Okello and Paul Muwanga was announced as the executive prime minister. At the swearing in of this regime, we heard on the radio, that former Ministers Kanyomozi, Samwiri Migwisa, and Amon Bazira were in attendance. On hearing this I decided that making the trek to Congo was not the best decision. I was just a mere member of parliament and wondered why I should run away, when the big shots were part of the new regime. So I decided to stay in my village of

Kyarumba until the situation was completely calm. My wife returned from the wedding and was at home. After one week I moved back to Kilembe to join my wife. The first trouble we encounter was the loss of our house as we were hauled into a small one bed room house. A soldier who identified himself as Bahindi carried out the operation of getting us out of the Kilembe mines houses. What happened was that as Tito Okello was sworn in as president he appealed to Yoweri Museven who was in Sweden at the time to come and join hands with him to rule Uganda after Obote. Museven while in Sweden was not too anxious to work with the Okellos. He had been fighting them for the last 4 years. So he called for negotiations while he ordered his men who were on the run in the west to consolidate their ground. They immediately captured Fort Portal and Kasese and organized massive recruitments. A lot of disgruntled UPDF soldiers who were tired of working with the Okellos, joined them. That is why we saw people like the Rev. Mutazindwa and NRA officer Bahindi taking control of Kasese under the command of Rwigyema and Kagame at the time. Museven consolidated his grip on the west by using Rwanda as the gateway. He called for peace talks while the Okellos now turned around and thought they would defeat him. President Daniel Arap Moi of Kenya offered to mediate in what many generally called the "peace jokes". They were peace jokes because Yoweri Museveni knew he was negotiating with a regime of illiterate generals with only one brilliant intellectual Minister of Foreign Affairs, Mr. Olara Otunu. While the peace talks were going on in Nairobi Museveni was busy acquiring territory by over-running all the cities in the west. His army grew up so fast and it was the most disciplined army Ugandans had seen in many days since Idi Amin left power. The west was peaceful while the central, which was controlled by the Okello soldiers, was in a mess; people were in misery, worse off than when Obote was in power. When Museven finally took Mbarara and was heading for Masaka, it became general knowledge that he was not interested in a peaceful settlement. He was not willing to share power with men he had fought with in Luwero partly because he did not want to explain much about the atrocities both armies committed against the people of Luwero and

Mubende districts. In fort Portal, Al hajji Musa Kigongo was in charge with a few carders helping him sort thing together. Hon. Chrispus Kiyonga returned from his exile home in Kenya and held one of the offices in Fort Portal. In February of 1985 I had visited Nairobi on business and had wanted to meet with Dr. Kiyonga on personal level. One of the things I wanted to discuss with him was that the UPC government was weakening every day by the conflict between the Langi and Acholis tribes in the army. I wanted to give him an inside story of what I knew after the death of David Oyite Ojok and perhaps find out what plans he had to return either to join us or whether he thought their bush war was making any progress that would provide a better alternative should there be a change of leadership between the Acholis and the Langis.

The contact I used from Campus Crusade to get to him reported back to me that Dr. Kiyonga will not meet with me because he feared I could be a spy wanting to kidnap him. Imagine simple civilian Member of Parliament as I was, to arrange a kidnap. This was not possible and not even something I would contemplate on doing. I lost an opportunity to connect with him for I found out later that he was very involved and connected as this became evident, when they took control of Kasese and Fort portal. I concluded that he was really well connected.

Do I regret having not seen him in Nairobi? No. Within 6 months the Okello Regime was overthrown and on January 26, 1986 Yoweri

Museveni declared himself president of the republic of Uganda. He announced a fundamental change with a 10-point program. He announced a cabinet of which the Bakonzo received their first full cabinet minister. Dr. Chrispus Kiyonga was appointed Minister of Corporative and Marketing. He later during several reshuffles occupied other prominent ministries like the Finance Ministry, the Internal Affairs Ministry, the Health Ministry [his profession], and now the Defense Ministry. When God gives, he gives in full. The Bakonzo had for a long time been crying for representation, God opened the door during this period when Museveni is president that their native Kiyonga has had the opportunity to occupy those prominent ministries deservingly since he was the only one who carried the banner of the UPM Party during the 1980 elections. There has often been talk in the corridor of power of people lining up to succession of the job of president. Amama Mbabazi who claimed that Besigye had jumped the queque first underscored this. Minister Otafirre later reiterated it. The man who should be close in the so-called lineup for the job should be Kiyonga, but has he shown interest? I don't think so because Kiyonga has not strived to have his life chronicled into the NRM's archives. He eschews the corridors of power by remaining the humble and loyal subject to His Excellency the President. He is the ultimate survivor in the regime where ministers have come and gone. He is the only Member of Parliament who has held 5 of the most powerful cabinet positions as well as the National Political commissar. He is in his own words and I quote "I was the only MP elected on the UPM ticket in 1980 that did not invalidate the cause for which I stood. On the contrary our thinking has blossomed in Uganda. In that case I am on record as the only MP who spear headed the growing of passion fruits and this has assisted many people all over Kasese. In Kampala if you want to get quality passion fruits you ask for those from Kasese. My struggle to revive cotton growing in Kasese is known to everybody. Being the only MP pushing this cause did not stop the fire catching on. I have scored a **first** in many other situations. That is leadership and I will continue leading the way in this regard". [New Vision Jan. 2005]

113

Dr. Kiyonga has had his positive contributions to the development of the district. Although he has been adamant and skeptical about the re-establishment of the Businga, he has articulated his reasons for rejecting the Omusinga while embracing the idea of the Obusnga. In the memorandum to the government he contends … on issue of integrity, politics and representation. …

The Omusinga Charles has often clashed with Dr. Kiyonga on public rallies as was evidenced on his return which attracted massive numbers of Bayira.

All in all, Dr. Kiyonga has remained a solid representative of his new constituency. At first he was Member of Parliament representing Kasese North, but when he came back from his exile life, he went to his native Bwera where he has carried out development projects to benefit the people. In 1980 Bwera had two political giants in the names of Amon Bazira and Dr. Henry Bwambale. In 1986 Dr.

Kiyonga prepared himself to be the next giant who would replace and carry on the development projects and all the unfinished business in Kasese west. In the 4 years Bazira was the representative, Bwera hospital was just a thought idea to be built on the Hill. Other ideas as put down by the local UPC committee were water, electricity and development of new schools. In 20 years Dr. Kiyonga has been the representative, Bwera has seen clean water, the hospital has been built and the schools started have been improved and upgraded. There has been improved security and communication overall. But let us not forget that this representative has held instrumental positions in government, thanks to H.E. Yoweri Museven for the confidence he has continued to bestow on this native son of Bwera. Obote did not do it the first time in 1962 – 70 or the second time 1980-84. The explanation the first time was the Bakonzo did not vote for UPC therefore he did not find anyone credible and educated enough to be appointed as a minister. The highest position held by a mukonzo was that of High commissioner to the UK. When Ezron Bwambale crossed from DP to UPC he was immediately appointed deputy minister of culture and community development. In 1980 there was a petition hanging on Amon Bazira filed by the Democratic Party. Obote explained that he did not want his government to be embarrassed if a cabinet minister lost the petition. Plus the elections in Kasese did not appear fair since there was news of misconduct at the returning officer's office. We did not lose the petition though, and Amon Bazira was never appointed Full minister in the four years Uganda Peoples Congress was in government. He however remained very powerful in security circles dating back from the time he was the director general of intelligence. His cabinet colleagues did not like him either because he was potentially fit for any of their portfolios in case the president decided on a reshuffle of his cabinet. Amon Bazira was assisinated in 1993 in Nairobi Kenya while wedging a liberation war against the NRM government. He was the head of NALU, the National Army for the Liberation of Uganda, a rebel movement that operated out of the Congo DRC. This rebel Army ceased to exist after he died in exile. The remnants joined the ADF, alied democratic forces, which were defeated by the government army in 1996.

CHAPTER 16

From Prison to Praise

In June 1986 when the NRM was fully in power, I did not see any chance of ever joining their political line. I decided to quit politics and start my own school in which my wife would be a teacher and I would be the sole proprietor. I had two vehicles, a salon car and a pick up truck. I decided to sell my salon Nissan datsun 120Y model to buy a second pickup truck. The reason for this was to use one truck in the construction of the school while the other was to be used for commercial purposes. I knew I would earn a living while constructing the school. I started carrying bricks. I laid a foundation for four classes and another for a staff house to house at least two teachers. Work was in progress in the whole month of June. My wife enrolled at Canon Apollo College to upgrade her skills to a grade three teacher. When she was gone for one week at canon Apolo College, I went down town Kasese on my way to the village where my bricks were being prepared. I stopped by the market and was approached by a tall man in plain clothes who introduced himself as John Doe for purposes of this book.. He asked me to drive him to the Kasese district court. He sat in the front seat of my small mini truck, a 120Y datsun pickup. I drove him to the court. As soon as we reached the court, he told me, "You are under arrest". I said, "For what?" He dragged me in the court and because he was such a tall giant, I did not resist. As if it was all stage managed, the magistrate was right there in his robes and read the charge to me. *"You are accused of Kidnap,* so you plead guilty or not guilty? In shock, I just replied, "not guilty" your honour Magistrate. "I m therefore directed to send you on remand at Mubuku prison right away". I told them I was not aware of the charges against me. They did not give me even a chance to talk to a lawyer nor inform my family. I drove my car with this tall man to Mubuku prison. To me this was the real kidnap; I was not allowed to leave my car with anybody. Everything appears to have been pre-arranged; I found the head of the prison institution, a senior superintendent of prisons waiting for me. He ordered one of the prison warders to register me, strip me of my civilian clothing and dress me with prison uniform which was infected with lice and dirty. Humiliated, undressed and now in prison dirty white cotton uniform, I complied and now I knew that the tall man was not joking, it was real and I was now prisoner. News circulated in Kasese town that I had been arrested and two people immediately came to see me while still at Mubuko prison. The first one was Mr. Yofesi Masereka who drove my small pick truck back home and the second one was the Bishop of south Rwenzori diocese. He prayed with me and promised that he would immediately travel to Fort Portal to get my wife from school to take care of family business. Her teaching career was now doomed and her two little boys' future was unpredictable. As well the school project was dead. My political career as a the youngest Member of Parliament had vanished with the coup the previous year. My whole life was turned upside down. *This was the long road God was preparing for me in order to transform me and to eventually turn me to Himself and begin to know and love Him.* **Phil. 1 vs. 6 says " he who started a good work in you will see to it that it is completed for the glory of His Kingdom."** *[Paraphrased from NIV]*

There was an immediate unrest in the prison quarters. Inmates were anxious to see me and were probably readying themselves to scold me or even whip me as the practice was. I stayed at what

I later came to know was the quarter guard; for more than two hours before I was allowed to join other remanded prisoners. There was unfounded rumor that the remnants of Rwenzururu rebels headed by Kinyamusitu; were going to storm the prison in order to forcefully release me. Because of this rumor I was quickly transferred to the notorious Katojo prison in Fort portal. This was considered maximum-security prison in Western Uganda. Two weeks later I was produced before the high court magistrate in Fort Portal and the same charges were read to me. I was again remanded to Katojo. Three weeks later Milton Bwambale, a former cadet in the army, joined me at Katojo. I did not know what charges were pressed on him. As soon as he got into katojo prison, he joined other notorious criminals and started planning an escape through the roof of the prison. One night he put his plans into action. He was living in a different wing from mine. I was only able to meet him during sunshine breaks. One night we heard gunshots at the prison, I thought, we were going to be killed. This was the time Milton and his group was trying to escape through the roof; they had opened the ceiling and three of them were up in the ceiling but were discovered by the night guard before they could jump off the roof. They were brought down, beaten, stripped naked and locked in a maximum-security cell. Life became extremely difficult after these kids attempted to escape. As a matter of fact this was the beginning of prison life because while out in the community as a high profile political figure you have no freedom because any time you know some military or cadre person would jump on you and administer mob justice on you especially if you did not agree to join their political line. However while in prison, you are protected by the prison authorities, in which case you are safer though not free. So when these disgruntled cadets tried to escape, freedom in prison was then denied to all of us. We were not given any food for two days, we were not allowed visitation and the entire prison was punished just because of the three chaps who wanted to escape. This escape was a blessing to me in disguise. Everything that happens in an explainable circumstance always happens for a purpose. God is always in situations when he wants to deliver those he loves. The prison authorities were scared of having high profile people like me and the army cadets under their protection without enough security.. An order came from the provincial prison authorities that we must be transferred to the Luzira maximum prison in Kampala. This was still a prison but a better prison, with the international community keeping their close eye on it. As a result of this attempted escape by those disgruntled chaps, we were transferred together with them to Kampala. In August, after two months in Katojo, we were transferred to Luzira. We traveled in a prison lorry with one Mutoro Lunatic whom they wanted to take to the mental hospital in Butabika. This lunatic old man made our trip to Luzira very enjoyable and humorous, as prisoners always were miserable. Each time we came across a trading center or a township, he could stand up and put his hands out through the lorry window; with shackle chains around his hands, and he would announce in the language of that township, the reasons why he is in shackles. For example when we passed through Fort Portal town he announced: *"bantwara, nyowe omukam wa toro, Ngu Nyangire okugura ekibiriti shilling 500"* [meaning: they have taken me, the king of toro, that I have refused to buy a match box at 500/-]. This man knew almost all the languages of the townships we travelled along the way from Fort Portal to Kampala. In Masaka, Lukaya and Lyantonde, he could say in Luganda that:*"bantute, Nze kabaka wa toro, ngu nagenye kugula ekibiriti sh. 500/-"*. In other words, he was saying that he had been arrested and now was being taken to Luzira for refusing to buy a matchbox at 500 shillings. Our trip was enjoyable because this lunatic man was entertaining us. At that time the NRM government had just devalued the Uganda shilling and a matchbox was alarmingly costing 500 shillings. This was not affordable to most low-income families. So this man was actually telling the truth, the reality of life outside our prison bars. When we arrived in Luzira, I found more former members of parliament, and former ministers who had been arrested on fictitious charges. At Luzira we learnt that it was common practice for the government to create a charge that would keep you in prison as long as possible so that you do not live among the population; unless you chose to join and support the government; then the leadership would not suspect you for political confusion. The NRM government was a new thing; they tried to introduce it as a party in 1980 i.e. UPM [Uganda Patriotic Movement] but could not get enough support to win more than one seat. When they went to the bush to fight the government, they did not have concrete evidence that the election was not free and fair. UPC did not defeat the leader himself. He was defeated by the Democratic Party, but did not sue the Democratic Party for defeating him; instead he went to the bush complaining that the election was not free and fair because he lost. Therefore any one who would explain to the people clearly that the Movement did not go to the bush because election was rigged, but went to the bush to fight their way to power, would be either eliminated or imprisoned. Such people were considered [kipingamizi] meaning saboteur. It was generally believed that if government removed anyone who would sabotage their campaign to introduce their "ten point program", the masses would readily accept them. That way, the ten point program which they sought to introduce after Museven was sworn in would find no resistance among the population. So right away, they came with a policy of eliminating any forms of opposition, so that when the NRM finally wanted to have elections, it would be the only political organization on the political playground. There were so many myths that surrounded the formation of the NRM leadership, for example the assertation that they went to the bush with 27 guns to fight the government would easily be defeated if it was explained clearly by a well informed political figure. The leader of the NRM was also the minister of Defense in the UNLF government, which means he could have had more than 27 guns. But this could not be explained to the population because whoever would explain this was either locked up in Luzira or had fled into exile.

In Luzira we were treated well, as political detainees. Nonetheless, the government made it a point to present us to the courts as the law stipulated so that the international community does not accuse the government of holding us without trial. They cleverly framed charges hard enough to prove beyond a reasonable doubt on either side; prosecution or defense; but would keep you remanded for as long as they wished. We were allowed to eat food from our homes prepared by people of our choice; because we had several enemies including some prisoners from the Amin era who were used as cooks. This was the only way to avoid eating poisoned food as was a rumored practice, and if you did, then your family will never know how you died. We were allowed to sleep on mattresses but on the floor sharing rooms with at least 4 others. We had a wing which they called the "politicians" wing. In this wing we lived with Chris Rwakasisi, Edward Rurangaranga, James Rwanyarare and Gashom Kagurusi. Lutakome Kayira, Dr. Henry Bwambale, Paul Muwanga, Lt. Namiti and Amon Bazira later joined us. A day after Amon Bazira arrive, we saw two lorries of "panda gari" prisoners who were picked up from the streets of Gulu and Kitgum. They called them loggers because they had no case to answer. They were paraded out side the prison office, journalist were called in and Amon Bazira was taken out of the prison and photographed with these loggers from the Northern Uganda. The next day's headline news carried a huge story that Amon Bazira had been brought in Luzira with rebels who were planning to over throw the government. When we heard this news in the press we were all amazed at how the authorities could lie to the public through the press and the entire country that Bazira belonged to the "panda gari" loggers now languishing in Luzira prisons. Most of these loggers died in this prison due to starvation and poor sleeping conditions. Every day, they were ferrying out of prison at least 3 bodies and this went on for more than three weeks without anyone raising a red flag. The news of constant dead bodies being brought out of Luzira leaked to the Red Cross. Red Cross came to visit and found the conditions very appalling. They made a strong submission to the international community and the government was put to task to improve the conditions of loggers whose rate of death had increased to almost five persons per day. These were human beings who were brought from northern Uganda, because they thought they would be easy recruits for the rebel armies especially that of Alice Lakwena's "Lord Resistance Army". This was the immediate major threat to the government after the fall of Kampala. The conditions for the loggers then improved and generally for all other prisoners. It is always tough for any new government to consolidate their authority especially when they were replacing what was considerer an elected and popular government. Of course they made several mistakes, which eventually they come to correct as they become comfortable with governance. In Luzira we were with many others prisoners most of whom were solders from both the defunct UPDF-Uganda People's Defense Forces, the Amin soldiers – Uganda Army, as well as some from the NRA – National resistance Army ranks who came in for discipline or/and spying purposes. One such soldier was a captain Rwamukaga who had shot and killed a former member of parliament in Bunyoro. As well some NRA soldiers who were responsible for indiscipline in the city were remanded in Luzira prison. We learnt more about their bush operations freely from them as some shared their bush stories and atrocities with us without fear because while in Luzira prison they did not know if they would be charged with criminal offences or whether they would be released and retain their jobs. So we collected free "bush" information as to how Yoweri Museveni and his army operated among the civilian population of the "famous Luwero triangle".

The NRM was careless as to how they threw their prisoner around prisons. In Luzira we found one prisoner of Pakistan citizenship, detained without charges, his name was Sajat. He told us he used to manufacture hand grenade and homemade bombs for the Kayira rebels and later for the Museven rebels. When Lutakome Kayira joined us at Luzira, he invited this Sajat fellow in his cell. We later learnt that Kayira was planning with Sajat to remotely organize rebel activities around the Rwenzori Mountains. This idea was opposed by Dr. Henry Bwambale and Amon Bazira both influential politicians from the Rewenzori mountains. Dr. Henry was a member of the Democratic party and while Bazira was a member of the Uganda Peoples congress party. They disagreed with Kayira about starting rebel activities from their homeland. Kayira was disappointed because he knew without the blessing of citizens from the area; a rebel movement would never succeed. I had never been so close to Kayira as this time in prison. I was able to see the three opposing politicians, Amon Bazira, Kayira and Henry Bwambale disagreeing in principal of starting a rebel movement together while they all agreed that the NRM government should be fought and removed. They did not know how this could be done since they were all in prison and had no access to freedom. Sajat was later released and deported. It is at this time that one afternoon; Lutakome Kayira and Paul Muwanga were sharing a meal together on their prison veranda that I joined them together with Henry Bwambale and Amon Bazira. We discussed generally why Ugandans tend to fight and kill each other. Kayira was a Muganda and had been fighting his fellow Muganda, Paul Muwanga when he was vice president of Uganda. Kayira asked for forgiveness from Paul Muwanga. I saw a reconciled Kayira. I saw Bazira reconciling with Dr. Henry Bwambale and asking for forgiveness for what happened during the 1980 elections, where Henry Bwambale was not allowed to be nominated as Democratic candidate. As we talked further about how to reconcile Ugandans, Kayira retorted; and he was speaking in Luganda; I quote: "Nze banage omusaja ono agenda kunzita". Meaning "my dear, this man is going to kill me". As if this was prophetically said, a week later Kayira was released from detention and within days, he was murdered in his home in Kampala. Of course Yoweri did not kill him, but an inquiry into his death that was ordered by President Yoweri Museven has never been made public. Scotland Yard was involved in the investigations, but still we have no results. After Kayira's death, a steady stream of bad news ensued. Paul Muwanga was released from dentition and later died in his home of illness which has never been explained. Lt. Namiti fell sick and was rushed to Mulago hospital. He later died there with unexplained circumstances.

Bazira and I kept a low profile while pursuing our cases with our lawyers without letting the press know. We believed that if the press knew of our maneuvers to fight our cases through the courts, the government would keep a tough eye on us. As it was the case in many times, people were re-arrested as soon as they left the court premises. We did not wish this to happen once we got releases.

October 27, 1987 I appeared before high court judge. He asked the government prosecutor to show reasonable cause why for 18 months they have not come to the high court to prove that there was a case to answer in my so called "kidnap" case. Because the government did not have enough evidence, the high court judge ordered that I be released on bail and gave the government 28 days to prove that there was a case to answer.

Life in Luzira

Life in Luzira was much better than that of Katojo were I was first kept as a maximum-security prison. We lived behind bars in a prison surrounded by a brick wall taller than building blocks we lived in. There was a football field as well as an arena where everyone could mix and mingle and play other indoor games. Our favorite game was scrabble. We were allowed visitation twice each week. One of my favorite hobbies while in this prison was reading, and the bible became one of my favorite books to read. I read about Kings in the bible, I read about Jesus and the forgiveness of sins. One of the things I discovered in the bible was that I had been a disobedient servant of the Lord almighty. I discovered that God creates us each for a specific purpose. And in the execution of our purposes, we ought to be pure and transparent. I began to see lots of faults in me that deserved punishment. As a young member of parliament, I was not transparent towards my family, my wife did not have enough time with me, and I paid more attention to constituency issues and other people than to my family. This was not right. Each time my wife came to visit, I saw her glittering eyes like I had never seen them before. She appeared more beautiful every time I looked at her through prison bars. After three months in this prison, I was allowed by the prison authorities to visit with my family members in a private room while watched at a distance by a warder. There were so many lessons I was learning each day I remained in prison. I began to feel sorry for the sins I had committed while I was Member of Parliament. I began to see how although I was rich, but yet I was poor in spirit. Material wealth started to weather away, because now I was at the mercy of ruthless warders while being watched over by the almighty God. I slowly began to realize that while I was a secular servant, I was disobedient to God to fulfill the purposes for which

I was created. I began to weep over my own sins as I read more and more of the holy Bible. So I literary surrendered my life to HIM and started to see things differently. I started to thank God even for allowing this to happen; because I was beginning to come to terms with reality. I saw how all people deserted me. I was no longer in position to help them therefore; there was no need even for them to see me in time of distress.

While in Luzira I was waiting upon the power of God to prevail. I secluded myself from other inmates one night and went into prayer by myself. It was 3:00 am on one morning night when I lit a candle and moved into the cell corridors so that I do not wake up other prisoners. Plus I did not want any prison warder to see light in our cell room while I was praying.

In that corridor, I opened my bible and read Jeremiah chapter 29:11…

When I saw what Lord told Jeremiah that he had plans for him, plans for a good future, plans for prosperity and not disaster. I prayed to the same God of Jeremiah. First I told this God that, I am not Jeremiah, but "if you lord have plans for me, just like you had for Jeremiah, then answer my prayers". This is what I told that God in my prayer in the prison cell corridor. "God, you know me by name. Even before I was born you already knew me. God even before I became the youngest Member of Parliament, you already knew me. God even before I came into this prison, you already knew, and you also know when I will get out of here. God I pray that you get me out of hear quickly so that I can fulfill the purposes for which you called me. Lord I know there many ways people get out of such prisons. They either escape, or there happens to be a coup and prisoners are released, or even better still, they go to court and are declared innocent and released. God if you can use one of these ways to get me out of here, "I will work for you to fulfill the purposes for which you called me by name". I pray this in the wonderful name of Jesus Christ. Amen". I concluded my simple prayer with a silent song of worship in the Rutoro hymn book number 123. I started praising the Lord and believing that freedom was a foot. It did not come right away. I spent another 4 months before I was produced before the high court judge. God chose the best way to set me free. It was not through escape, neither was it through a coup de etat. The government for which I wished the coup still rules today and may probably be there for another 10 or so year. God in his infinite wisdom reigned over my fears, led me through prison towards praise. After Luzira, I stayed in Kampala for two weeks before I moved to my hometown. I first went to the central police station to report, and there I encountered no problem at all. The good Lord was with me.

CHAPTER 17

The Ultimate Escape

December 27, 1987 was the day I made a real escape. News came to my house in Kilembe that military intelligence personnel were in town and were wondering whether a former member of parliament who recently got out of luzira was still in Kampala. Their informer actually misinformed them and reported that I was not in Kampala but I was in my home village of Kyarumba visiting parents and relatives.

The same informer hired a taxi and drove to my house in Kilembe to come and tell me of what was a foot. He said, "Men in civilian clothes were in town on mission to pick you up and detain you in a military prison". The military prisons as we knew them were more of torture chambers than actually prison cells. People there were living a life of torment and deep suffering, which resulted in most cases death. I couldn't envisage my self getting into torture chambers after gaining my freedom from Luzira. I knew God was with me and I also knew that it was God who sent this informer to tip me of what was eminent. I did not take anything for granted. I told my wife to once again take courage and stay alone. I told her, that she had endured tough times while I was in Luzira. I did not want her to face the same yet again if I was unfortunate enough to join those in military cells. This was where there was reported gross abuse of human rights. These were places where Red Cross was never allowed to visit. These were places like the notorious Basima house where the international community would never be told what was going on there. I had to elude this, by quickly stepping out and convincing my wife that God will take care of her with her two little kids, and that he would take care of me as I go into the unknown. I told her, that as long as I was alive, God will take care of us, and will reunite us to serve him. I kissed her goodbye and headed for the nearest boarder. A good friend of mine played the roll of a Good Samaritan. He gave me his car; I traveled through the main road passing through roadblocks without being detected. Later at night I crossed the border into Congo, which was then called Zaire. This was the escape. I was met at the boarder post in Zaire by a military colonel who was in charge of that area. At the time there were insurgents fighting to remove the government of the then President Mubutu Sese Seko of Zaire. These insurgents were having hideouts in Uganda. As soon as I sat in the military helicopter, I knew that I had gotten myself out of Uganda, and that my escape had been successfully executed. The helicopter dropped me in a small town called Beni in a military barracks. Four days later, government agents transported me to the city of Goma where I was handed over to immigration. Asylum was processed and a united high commissioner for refugees' card was issued to me. I was then left to vend for myself in a town I had no clue how thing were done. I could not speak French. If I wanted to teach English, I was required to know some French or better still some Swahili. It was going to be difficult to get a job in this town, I told my self. My hotel expense account was over, I was required to pay or check out. I actually checked out and found myself under the care of the Goma CPZA church. This was a community of churches under the Pentecostal assemblies of Zaire. The pastor here inquired of me if I would be willing to wake up at 5:00am to pray with the rest of the staff. I said yes, and I knew that God answers prayers. I stayed at this church for seven days, and when I moved out, I made this my regular church. I prepared my self for a life of uncertainties.

I continued to pray that God will take care of my family in Uganda, and enable them to join me. With God's help I was able to find some one who regularly traveled to Uganda, and became the link to my family.

We connected with my family and agreed that we reunite and live together though in a foreign land, we would seek God's guidance. My wife moved into Zaire living behind a country she served as a teacher and young women's Christian association outreach worker. She came to a country where she neither knew the official language, French nor the local language Swahili. She depended on her capacity to learn and adapt. Strong willed as she was, she started what were to become the worst days of her life. She had lost her status as a wife of a former member of parliament, she had lost her civil life as a teacher and now she would be subjected to a village life, full of suffering, and uncertainties. With the little money she came with from her country, we were able to rent one little town house for one year. We were able to save some money for food on a regular basis. We could not afford to put our son in preschool. We joined a prayer group headed by a lady – mama Feza, who not only was a parent, but she became a spiritual mother. She prayed for us, and gave prophesies about what God had in store for us if we can only trust in him. She was an encouraging spiritual leader and we enjoyed being part of her prayer group. Amon Bazira who had been released in early January 1988 joined us in Goma. We did not immediately know the circumstances under which he left the country. He joined us in the prayer group and at one time we agreed with each other that if we should ever go back to Uganda, a prayer group like this one, where people came for healing, restoration and salvation, should be introduced in our communities. **Prayer centers** where people came to seek the living God was what was lacking in Uganda. The country had become morally corrupt and needed God even through the leadership. Our money was running out and life was increasingly becoming tough to manage. We decide to leave Goma immediately and migrate to Beni where we could be close to relatives and friends. Amon Bazira on his part moved to Kinshasa and was being looked after by the Mubuto government. In Beni we spoke the same language. After we moved into Beni, a movement called NALU headed by Amon Bazira was formed. There were disturbances along the Zaire and Uganda boarders. As we got more squeezed with hunger and no money, we were contemplating going back to our Land and face the real tortures in the military; but God said no. There was confusion in Uganda about the existence of rebels along the boarder. In fact there were no rebels as such. The name NALU was so scary that people thought Amon Bazira had mercenaries and that the Zairian army was backing him. This was a total misrepresentation of situation. NALU was just myth at this time. There was to be no war, as Amon and Henry had prevented Kayira from staging rebel activities along the Rwenzori Mountains. Bazira was not about to make the same mistake. But it was common knowledge that war was imminent and when army offers from the government defected into Congo so that they could join the "imaginary NALU" army, they were unceremoniously disappointed because they had believed a pack of lies about the existence of an army with mercenaries that was ready to remove Museven from power. These lies about the existence of an army called NALU actually motivated Bazira to seek help from Mubutu and Arap Moi to fight against the National Resistance Movement. Bazira did not live to see this army in action as he died in 1983 and thereafter that army that was still mysterious vanished. Museven still rules today and there has been chunks of such lies over the years beginning from Lakwena in the north, to Peter Otai in the East and to Itongwa in the central as well as Tubliqs ADF in the west. There was the "Kirimutu group" in Bunganda for which Dr. Henry had been implicated and detained. There is still the "Lord Resistance Army" in the north that has caused untold suffering to the people of Acholi land. All these groups have come and gone living the civilian population in turmoil. People have had breaking hearts, absolutely dominated by sadness and deep frustrations as they continue to see their children get abducted and forced to join useless armies in a bid to oust the sitting government. It has not worked and may not work in years to come. The days of rebel activities expired in the 1986 and now we have democratic practices remaining to be the basis for removing a government. In acholi land we have heard of untold suffering by children who walk day and night looking for safe havens. They have nicknamed them "night commuters". This did not happen before the double Okellos ignored democratic practice to remove a government.

And now while the authorities in the border town of Beni were awaiting instructions from Kinshasa, the capital of Congo, the Ugandan deserters were told to hold on here until word came from Kinshasa to decide their fate. They had wanted to climb the mountains to hide in the forest until Amon Bazira came. I told Major Kapuchu and Major Patrick Muhindo that if they had come to join Bazira's Army, there was none and that they were "now the army". I also told them that going to the mountains would be futile for the people of Kasese where they came from. Amon himself had not invited them because he had nothing on the ground to warrant fighting a government, which was increasingly becoming popular with the people. Meanwhile I had wanted to travel to Kinshasa, and had failed to get money enough to buy a ticket. I believed in my heart that if God allowed me get out of luzira, he would enable me to reach Kinshasa where I could be able to speak English because this was a capital city were embassies were located and most of the people there spoke some English. I hoped to look for employment in the capital while seeking to move out for resettlement.

An opportunity came knocking on my door for me to travel to the capital with the deserters. An order had come from the Military in Kinshasa that the fugitives from Uganda should not be allowed to live by the boarder as they were intending to stage military operations against a neighboring country. I did not know that they were under arrest. They had crossed the border illegally. But the good news for them was that Uganda and Congo did not have extradition treaty. So although they were under arrest, they would not be deported. They were to be moved away from the boarder so that they do not cause bitterness and suffering along the common border. I was requested by the 'commission de zone' of this local town to accompany this team to the capital and to help explain why they crossed the border in the manner in which they came. Spontaneously I grabbed the opportunity and accepted the offer. I was to travel to the capital, free of charge in an army transport plane. What a blessing, I thought to myself. This had been my dream and I had almost lost faith in prayer. My wife did not lose faith though for she continued to intercede on behalf of the entire family.

The day came when we were to board the plane to Kinshasa. The instructions were that they were picking up eight fugitives but the commissioner de zone presented nine people. They did not appear to be bothered by the extra person. I was happy that they did not. We happily jumped into the military transport plane, a C130. After five hours of flight, we landed in a military airport called Ndolo. A prisons truck was waiting with instruction to pick up eight [8] Ugandan fugitives but was dismayed to see nine. They had no choice but to take all the nine. I was number 9 and was not a fugitive, but they took me with them anyways. It was at this point that we realized that we were getting into a military jail. The unpredictable reality had again kicked in. We headed for a short but painful jail term. Freedom was again snatched and this time in a foreign land.

CHAPTER 18

From Freedom to prison – second episode.

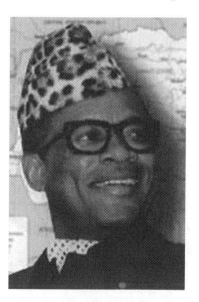

The Democratic Republic of Congo is a vast country with close to zero communication networks. At the time we lived there between 1987 and 1992 it was called Zaire, led by the notorious dictator

Mubutu Sese Seko Kuku Gwendu wa Zabanga. He was a close friend of Idi Amin. He and his MPR leaders had amassed great wealth abroad, which left the country empty of social infrastructure. Mubutu had been the darling of the west since he took over power from the Belgians. Belgium's king Leopold had treated Congo as his personal business property. As long as Mubutu promised the Western imperialists, that he would prevent communism from setting foot on the African soil, his gross violation of human rights was ignored. He committed many crimes against his own people, including denying them the basic rights to civilization and basic infrastructure. There is no road that will lead you from one city in the west to another in the east. For example you can only fly from Goma in order to get to Kinshasa. To get to Kisangani from Goma by road you need at least one to two weeks of truck driving. The few existing roads are horribly dilapidated with deep potholes and overgrown bushes.

When we arrived in Kinshasa it appeared as if we had entered another country altogether. We saw a city, with a population of more than 4 million people with trenches of water uncared for. With sky scrapers and roads with overpasses and with a monument structure unfinished and which might never be finished. Mubutu was a small lord on the African soil. He controlled other leaders like Habyaliman of Rwanda and Buyoya of Burundi. They were like his classroom monitors while he was the head prefect. But once communism crumbled, taking Mubutu's usefulness with it, his external support from America and Europe evaporated. Military vehicles and aircrafts crowded the military airport where we landed. We entered his country during his last days when his grip on power both in his country and his controlled neigbouring countries was slipping. Wide spread anarchy was the order of the day. His own military gurus were denuding the country left and right, and discontent in the army was prevalent. We could feel it as we arrived in the capital Kinshasa. Widespread demonstrations were evidenced in streets and at the University of Kinshasa. We were ordered to move two by two into a prisons truck. One of the fugitives, Major Muhindo tried to resist. He told the military officer on site that, I quote; "we are military personnel from Uganda, and we should not be under arrest". The man clearly replied in Lingala language, quote; "*yo. Kanga munoko, awa ezali Uganda tee*" meaning, "you shut up your probosis, this is not Uganda." At this point I knew for sure that we had been denied our freedom and we were going to be confined to yet another prison, this time in a foreign land. I did not know what to expect. We were driven for about 30 minutes into a military prison. We found in this prison military officer who had been lockup for indiscipline and others with various crimes ranging from corruption to treason. They had access to television news, and were allowed newspapers. They slept on beds like school dormitories, and ate food from their homes. One of us lamented, "this is not bad". While in this prison, we were informed by the military officer in charge that we were ordered to come here because Uganda was seeking the extradition of the eight fugitive soldiers. We even saw on National television Ugandan President Museven meeting with his Zairian host President Mubutu at his Gbadolite resort home, the equivalent of 'rwakitura'. At the meeting they discussed bilateral issues ranging from boarder security, trade, refuges, and behind closed doors we were told, that Mubutu told Museven emphatically that he cannot hand over any refugee who seeks asylum in his country. We are told that it is at this meeting that Museven developed deep hatred for Mubutu and vowed to assist anyone who would over throw him. Museven did not trust Mubutu and he now knew that his boarder on the west would never be secure as long as Mubutu was in control in Kinshasa. Mubutu's down fall started right here as Laurent Kabila's ragtag rebels who were scatted all over East Africa started to swallow their saliva, because it would not be long before Yoweri Museven gave them full support to erase the dictator from the face of the planet and drive Congo into deeper turmoil as they plunder the leftovers. The support of Kabila by Yoweri Museven did not only culminate in a security measure along the common boarder; it exposed a commercial enterprise by both Uganda and Rwanda, so ruthless in its design and so pitiless in its implementation that resulted in the extermination of millions of people in the North and South Kivu provinces. Under the disguise of securing common boarders of Uganda and Rwanda, and riding them of rebels and bandits, Uganda and Rwandan soldiers amassed

135

tremendous wealth from Congo's timber, gold, diamonds, and other precious minerals. The United States and United Nations just kept mum and turned a blind eye as they did in 1994 when Rwandese were busy massacring each other in what has come to be known as the worst genocide of modern times. People who speak the same language decimated almost one million people; just because others were Tustsi and other were Hutu.

Once Mubutu Sese Seku died in 1997, his giant country seemed to have died with him as was described by Madeleine Drohan in her book, making a Killing. She contends, "The foreign armies were not the only vultures feeding off the corpse of the Congo. They worked alongside and sometimes in concert with criminal groups, arms traffickers, diamond smugglers rebel groups and companies that saw the potential for profit in a conflict zone."[Drohan 291]

After Museven had gone back to Kampala Amon Bazira was arrested in Rwanda by the Habyalimana government. They wanted to trade him for their own fugitives who were in Uganda. Hyabyalimana and Mubutu were great friends, when Mubutu's security staff in Goma heard that a Uganda high profile rebel leader was being held in Kigali, they rushed in to rescue him and immediately rushed him into Kinshasa. A district delegation left Kasese to demand that Bazira be arrested and handed over to Uganda, because he was going to cause trouble at the boarder by starting a movement which would threaten the stability of Uganda. This delegation included the then District RC5. They met with their counter parts in Beni, and were told that Kinshasa had arrested the fugitives and their leader and all would be handed over. They were deceived. They went back to Bwera with what they considered good news and held rallies at Mpodwe and Kasese claiming that Bazira was going to be handed over to them. There were jubilations all over the district with members of parliament and other local leaders celebrating what later became a hoax. They had been lied to, and this backfired. Bazira was at loose, and indeed he became a thorn in the side of the government. It was common knowledge that if he started a movement, he would attract a huge number of following. As he was trotting between Kinshasa and Nairobi, the long arm of NRM security operatives caught up with him and in 1993 his body was found on one of Kenya's highway. An inquiry into his death by the Kenya government has never been ordered and we may never know the circumstance under which he died. The Kasese population for whom he served as Member of Parliament still misses him.

Three weeks later, we were transferred from the military prison to a worse detention centre. The special intelligence unit called A.N.D- agence nationale de defance manned this. In this place we were treated like real criminals, we were not given regular meals, we were not allowed to take regular baths and we were only allowed out on the sun shine once a day for only one hour.

Our freedom was taken away. We were told we mounted to nothing because we came from a country that had haboured insurgents for many year fighting against the government of President Mobutu. After spending three weeks of untold suffering here, we were visited by a group of Red Cross officials. When they came to me I showed them my identifications, and they wondered why I was here. They immediately contacted the United Nations High commissioner for Refugees because I held their card which was issued to me in Goma when I first landed.

The next day they came back with a staff from the United High Commissioner to rescue me. The Red Cross pleaded for the other eight fugitives to be rescued as well. We were all released from this dungeon and handed over to the UNHCR.

In the mean time, my spouse who appears abandoned and frustrated was having the greatest share of shame and suffering. She was lonely and living a life of scorn even by kids. She was trying to unload the double and often multiple yoke on her back as she was taking care of two little people. She was living with strangers who turned to be family in the long run. Through her religious medium of prayer, she called out for help. In her own solitary confinement in a room of prayer, she often yelled to an invisible God and the scorn came from the neigbours and children as to when that invisible God will hear her cry. Like the average rural woman she had become, whose dilemma she often internalized, she calls for spiritual help to balance her load like her rural counter parts; that had become part of her life in the prayer group. They had become like her traditional sisters. This relationship was to last into an everlasting friendship and sisterhood. Apart from being domestically discouraged, she did not lose the spirit of trusting in the invisible living God, who ultimately answered her call for help in the long run. While for the four years she lived without my intimate relationship, she was almost fully integrated into the African rural culture although she lived with the stigma in the periphery of the high social class she had just been ejected out of; a high table classic social class of women of status.

In Kinshasa, the UNHCR settled us into a transitional house in one of the busy neigbourhoods of the city. We were free at last.

As we lingered around the capital, free at last, we saw opportunities for resettlement knock on our doors of hope. As I visited various embassies and high commissions in Kinshasa, I came to know how people get resettled in other countries. I spoke to the fugitives that we need to find a way out of this congested massive city. Everyone in the group had different ambitions. It is at this point that I realized God had sent them across the border not to come and cause trouble, but to air lift me from the rural life of suffering to the city life of opportunities and hope. God indeed created a way, where there was no way. As for them, they one by one returned to Uganda through various ways. They refused my idea of seeking resettlement to another country. Some of them actually fulfilled their desire to go into the bush to fight but when they realized that the bush was empty, they surrendered. Others just went straight back. One can only conclude that there was a divine push for them to cross the border but they did not know the actual motive. Only God did. It was all spiritually motivated. God had a purpose for our lives, and the work he had started in us, had to be accomplished through us, by Him. Phil.1: 6. The good work of initiating schools to enhance literacy in the Ruwenzori had to be finished. And as he says, in John 15:16 that we did not chose him, but he chose us, to bear fruit, fruit that will last for generations to enjoy. A way had to be found in which our lives could be preserved so that our works would glorify his name.

So as the group of fugitives left, I used my crudely earned freedom to continuously visit various embassies in the capital to pressurize for resettlement. I forgot for a little that I had a family far away in the interior although I knew for a fact that even if I did remember, there was no way I could get in touch with them. It was like I was in another exile, and I felt sorry for my wife who continued to endure the pressure of shame by herself without me at her side. I even forgot for a while that I had prayed in Luzira for God to grant me freedom in order to work for him. The UNHCR was not willing to find a place for me in a third country. They urged that my life was not in any danger. I however ignored them and moved to visit various embassies. The British embassy in Kinshasa was my immediate target.

I spoke to the immigration counselor named Schneider. I had received this reference from my long old friend Tom Stacey from UK who had advised me to talk to Mr. Schneider [*not real name*] and ask about the possibility of migrating to the UK. I was told here that Britain was more sympathetic to the Museven government; therefore they would not be accepting people running away from Uganda. They considered Uganda safe enough for all people to live. They did not get my point. I was however able to convince him that Uganda was not suitable for me at this point after narrating all that had happened. He gave me his card and asked me to visit the protection officer at the UNHCR. He wanted the protection office to call him so that they discuss options for me to get out of the Congo. The protection officer on seeing that I had moved way beyond their sphere of influence did not call him. He just confined himself to his sphere of influence, gave me application forms and assured me that they will find a country for me. Within days, I was scheduled to attend three interviews; Canada, USA and Australia. I chose to attend the Canadian interview first, and at the end of the interview, the immigration officer who had traveled from Abidjan, Ivory Coast, told me that I had passed the interview and would be resettled into Canada. He requested for my family to be brought from interior upcountry of Congo, into the capital to join me as we prepare to journey into the country of the maple leaf, Canada. The

UNHCR made immediate arrangements to bring my family. They prepared air tickets for all my family including the 7 year old son who was still in Uganda.

My wife who had felt abandoned for a while, but not by God finally reunited with me and we were a complete set. We went through the immigration procedures of the Canadian embassy, a process that took almost two year. In this waiting process, we were able to make a fourth child to conclude our number to six. At the time of departure, we received a test of faith. God sent one friend of ours to bid us farewell and delivered to us five [5] US dollars to go with to Canada. This friend had his son in the United States and wanted me to buy stamps to mail a letter to his son. We did not know that 5 dollars was a blessing that would carry us into the unknown and prosper us to turn our eyes to God and listen to what he has destined us to do. The works he started in us even before we knew him intimately had to be accomplished. We have just started. More lay ahead, dealing with people's attitudes, the spirit of reconciliation among the entire people referred to in this reading. Forgiveness builds strong bridges. The traumatic situations and conditions our whole family was subjected to during this whole journey. God prepared us to travel this far to examine with other immigrants different aspects of life. As well to use our experiences to help others in similar traumatic circumstances.

I have written this biographical and factual truth as a subject of my own narrative, witnesses to and participants in my own experience, and in no way coincidentally in the experiences of those with whom I have come in contact. I have wished that people do not read imaginative literature either by us or about us from a stand point of view of fiction. You need to hear the true story. And you have to read it from the one who lived it. Lest you forget.

EPLOGUE

The Unforgetable myth became REAL

On October 19, 2009 Charles Wisley Irema Ngoma was celebrating what was called the 43rd coronation anniversary. The president of Uganda Yoweri Museveni was present and one of the most important announcements he made was to recognize the existence of the Rwenzururu Kingdom, which had been the subject of a bitter struggle for many years. At a colorful ceremony at the Kilembe Mines Gold Club, more than 30,000 people came to witness the recognition of the Obusinga. Delegations of high ranking officials came from the Democratic Repoblic of Congo where the Bayira number to almost 5millions as opposed to about 1 million in Uganda. The myth that kept the people together as they collectively fought for what was inherently theirs came to real life. In recent years there had been oppositions to the recognition of this institution. Various insignificant kings have masquaraded as rightful kings. Politicians of various political parties had hoped that these mashrooming would be kings would pull support from the indigenous people in Kasese and Bundibugyo, but the rightful King who had lived in the United States for over 25 years prevailed. A new Rwenzururu anthem was played on that day. It is on record as the best melodious anthem of modern times. The anthem tells the story of what Rwenzururu kingdom is all about.

Omusinga/King Charles Wesley Mumbere with Queen Agnes Mumbere on the morning of the 43rd anniversary of Rwenzururu Kingdom. On this day October 19, President Yoweri Museveni and Dr. Chrispus Kiyonga, addressed Mumbere as 'His Majesty Omusinga Irema-Ngoma' for the first time. GLORY BE TO THE ALMIGHTY GOD THAT WE CAN SEE THIS IN REAL LIFE TIME.

THE REAL BUHIKIRA ROYAL PALACE – KASESE TOWN